More Advance Praise for *Happiness Is Free*

"In his great book, *Happiness Is Free, and It's Easier Than You Think**, Hale Dwoskin continues the lifelong work and teachings of the great Lester Levenson, and has written a 'do-it-yourself', 'easier than you think,' Method that has transformed lives worldwide! With the information and exercises learned from this book, you will be able to let go of all that keeps you from living a life free from all limitations and live a life of happiness, joy and peace."

Diana Nightingale, Owner, Keys Publishing, Inc., international speaker, and author of *Learning To Fly As A Nightingale*

"*Happiness is Free* presents a psycho-spiritual perspective that applies the most esoteric wisdom to everyday human misery–and in a way that feels both practical and stunning, shows us how to move beyond insight and actually release what ails us. I am very grateful."

Nancy Dreyfus, Psy.D. author of *Talk To Me Like I'm Someone You Love: FlashCards for Real Life.*

"Stop Striving!! Learn to 'Let it Happen', not 'Make it Happen.' Hale and Lester, two 'master teachers' teach you a truly effortless way to a great life through the simple principles outlined in *Happiness Is Free*. These simple techniques can change your life–FOREVER! What we learned in a four-day class in 1991 has been concisely synthesized in this wonderful, instructional book. You will actually discover how to stop being your own strongest barrier to success. Within months of learning Lester's principles we began to reach personal, professional, and spiritual heights we had never known existed. We heartily recommend that you learn it for yourself. Because Happiness IS Free, and it really IS easier than you think."

Barbara Mark & Trudy Griswold, authors of *Angelspeake Trilogy and Heaven & Beyond: Conversations with Souls in Transition*

"In these times of turmoil and uncertainty, the simple yet profound truths expressed by Lester Levenson provide a powerful backdrop against which the events of our lives and our world can be seen and understood from an expanded perspective, bringing clarity and peacefulness in its wake. The commentaries provided by Hale Dwoskin help to build a bridge between the understanding of Lester's words and the organic integration of his wisdom into the day-to-day activities of our daily lives. For those already familiar with Lester's thoughts and with releasing, these volumes will bring additional depth and clarity to their understanding and practice. For those unfamiliar with Lester or his work, these volumes have the potential to be the doorway to a new way of looking at the world."

Elliott Grumer, Psychiatrist, Phoenix, AZ

*Advance Praise For *Happiness Is Free* Book One

Happiness Is Free

... and it's easier than you think!

Book 4

by Hale Dwoskin
& Lester Levenson

Sedona
Training Associates

Printed in the U.S.A. by Malloy Inc. on acid free 85% recycled paper.

Publisher:

Sedona Training Associates
60 Tortilla Drive, Suite 2
Sedona, AZ 86336
Phone: (928) 282-3522
Fax: (928) 203-0602
E-mail: release@sedona.com
Web: www.sedona.com

Cover design and illustration by Lightbourne © 2001
Interior book design by Wendy Barratt

Library of Congress Number:
ISBN 0-915721-03-1
Set of 5 books ISBN 0-915721-05-8
Special pre-publication limited edition.

To all seekers and finders

of the ultimate happiness everywhere

and Sedona Method® graduates

worldwide

Acknowledgments

I would like to thank the following people for making this book possible: My loving wife, Amy Edwards, all Sedona Method® graduates worldwide, Stephanie Gunning, Sara Whitcomb, Diane Brace, as well as all of the Sedona Training Associates staff.

Table of Contents

Lester Levenson

Happiness Is Free

... and it's easier than you think!

Book 4

Publisher's Note

If you have read any of the other books in this series, you will probably notice that the Introduction and How to Gain the Maximum Benefit from This Book sections are the same in each volume. This is done intentionally so that you can review them with each reading. If you have already read these chapters several times, you can choose to skip directly to the first session when exploring this book.

The Next Steps and Guidelines for *Happiness Is Free* Support Groups are also repeats. They are provided in this book for your convenient reference.

Introduction

What Is Happiness?

Quite simply put, happiness is you being your Self. Not the limited self that you pretend to be most of the time, but the unlimited Self that you are and have always been. This is the Self that is always effortlessly present before, during, and after everything else that appears in your experience. You are the radiant yet changeless background that allows for everything else to exist.

If that is true, you may be wondering, why is it so hard to discover and why have there been so many books written on the topic–including this one? The answer to that is not as simple.

We have spent eons pretending to be anything but unlimited. In fact, we have become so good at this pretending to be limited that we have forgotten that it is just a game, a pretense. We now spend most of our time bolstering the illusion that we have created for ourselves, leaving very little time for the inner reflection that can set us free from this totally self-imposed and artificial sense of limitation.

It takes tremendous energy to maintain the illusion that

unlimited Beingness is actually limited to the particular body-mind that you call yourself. No wonder we are so exhausted most of the time. We have unlimited energy available to us, but instead of using this energy for good or to discover who we truly are, we use this energy to convince ourselves and others around us that we are limited–that we have personal problems.

The late Lester Levenson, my friend and the coauthor of this book, used to say that extraditing ourselves from this situation in which we all find ourselves is either "simple or impossible." It is simple when we allow it to be easy. We can allow our energy to flow inwards towards self-discovery and for loving acceptance of what is. It is impossible when we force our energy to flow outwards. We fight against the world of our own creation and try to prove to everyone, including ourselves, that our world and its problems are real.

Are you ready to make it simple? You probably are if you were attracted to read this book. This book is designed to guide you experientially to rediscover your ultimate happiness by uncovering the real unlimited you.

The happiness that is you is totally independent of what you have or do not have, yet it improves your experience of whatever you have or don't have. This happiness that is you is also independent of what you do or do not do, yet it makes your experience of whatever you do or don't do more enjoyable. This happiness really is who you are, and you can experience it for yourself by reading this book and following the simple suggestions contained within it.

I know that you have probably heard promises like these before. And you may have often been disappointed. Which, of course, could make you a little skeptical. If you are in doubt, that is okay. I encourage you to believe nothing that you read in this book until you can prove it for yourself. But I promise you that this program is different. I have the absolute conviction that you can uncover your ultimate happiness and live it in every moment. This conviction is based on my own direct experience over the last quarter century of working with Lester Levenson and his teachings and then sharing them with thousands of people around the world.

Yet I did not always feel convinced. I met Lester Levenson in 1976. Back then I was an ardent, although confused seeker who had gone to many trainings and seminars led by teachers from both the East and the West. I had studied various body-centered disciplines, including Yoga, Tai Chi, and Shiatsu. I had actively participated in various courses, including EST, Actualism, Theta Seminars, and Rebirthing. I had many nice experiences at these seminars, and heard and understood–at least intellectually–many useful concepts. Still I felt incomplete. I longed for a simple and powerful answer to some important, yet vexing questions like: "What is my life's purpose?" "What is truth?" and "Who am I?"

Much of what I had heard and experienced only added to my questioning. No one seemed to have truly satisfying answers or have truly satisfied him or herself about what their true nature was or what was the ultimate truth. There was also a strong, almost universal belief that growing was hard work and required baring your soul and reliving painful, unresolved issues. However, that all changed during a very fortunate encounter with a remarkable man.

I met Lester at a seminar that I had organized for a well-known speaker, which Lester attended as the seminar leader's guest. That day, a group of us went out to lunch together, where Lester's presence immediately struck me as special. He was in total peace and equal-mindedness, very comfortable with himself. He was unassuming and easy to talk to, and treated everyone as his friend—even me, a complete stranger. It was obvious that he had ended his search by discovering the answers I'd been seeking. I knew I had to find out more.

When I asked Lester what he did, he invited me to a seminar that was being held the next weekend. All he would tell me about it was that, "a group of people is going to sit around a table and release." I wasn't sure what that meant, but I knew if it could even point me in the direction of the qualities of which Lester was the living embodiment, I definitely wanted it. I took a leap of faith and signed up on the spot.

Almost overnight I knew that I had found what I was looking for. In fact, deep inside I knew that this process of releasing and Lester's teachings were what I had been born to do and share with the world—and to this day I have never wavered.

Before we move on to explore more of what you can expect from this book, I would like to share Lester's story with you in his own words. The quote that follows is very similar to the story that Lester unfolded for me shortly after I met him and started exploring his teachings:

I was born July 19, 1909, in Elizabeth, New Jersey, into a middle class family as a very shy person. I tried to do things the way they were supposed to be done—doing the right thing, getting a good education, and being the best in my field. My natural inclination was towards science, especially the science of the world, and of man himself. I graduated from Rutgers University in 1931 as a physicist, after which I worked twenty-some years in physics and engineering.

In physics, I worked in research and development on measuring instruments and automatic control, connected with Brown Instrument Co., which later became a subsidiary of Honeywell. And in the engineering field, I worked as a mechanical engineer, an electrical engineer, a construction engineer, a heating and venting engineer, and a marine engineer–actually, fourteen different fields.

I also went into various businesses, including restaurants, lumber, building, and oil, intertwined with engineering, wanting to make money, wanting to make it in the world. At that time, I did not know what I now know–that what I was seeking was actually the answers to life itself. Nothing that I had worked at would give me that answer, and as the years went by, I became heavy with depression and with sickness.

By 1952, I had been through constant illness–I even had jaundice three or so times a year. I had an enlarged liver, kidney stones, spleen trouble, hyper- and hypo-acidity, ulcers that perforated and formed lesions, and to top it off, I had at least ten years of migraine headaches. This all culminated in 1952 when I had my second coronary thrombosis.

After the second coronary, I was told I would not live much longer–that I might die any day and shouldn't make the effort to take so much as a step unless I necessarily had to. I was extremely fearful of dying, but I said to myself, "You're still breathing, Lester–there is still a chance." So I sat down and began thinking on an "around the clock" basis. Having lived forty-two or so years, and having reached the end of the line without happiness, without health, I realized that all the knowledge I had accumulated was of no avail. I had studied Watson's behaviorism in the 30's and Freud's in the late 30's and early 40's. I had studied the philosophies. I had studied logic. I studied economics. I studied all the major fields of man, and with all that knowledge there, I was at the end of the line. This made me realize that the accumulated knowledge of man was of no use.

So I decided to start from scratch. Forget all that knowledge. Begin from point zero and see what you can pick up. So, I posed the questions, "What am I?" "What is this World?" "What is my relationship to it?" "What is Mind?" "What is Intelligence?" "What is Happiness?"

I began by asking myself, "What do I want out of life?" And the answer was happiness. Investigating further, I went into the moment when I was feeling happiest. I discovered something which to me was startling at the time. It was when I was loving that I was happiest. That happiness equated to my capacity to love rather than to being loved. That was a starting point.

I began correcting all my thoughts and feelings in that direction from that of wanting to be loved, to that of loving. And in that process, I discovered another major thing that kind of shocked me. I saw that I wanted to change this entire world, and that was the cause of my ulcers–or one of the major causes. In realizing how much I wanted to change things in this world, I saw how it made me a slave of this world, I made the decision to reverse that. And in the process of following out these two directions–actually unloading all the subconscious concepts and pressures in those directions–I discovered I was getting happier, freer, lighter, and feeling better in general.

As I saw this direction was good, I made the decision that if a slice of pie tasted this good, I wanted the whole pie. And I decided not to let go of this direction until I got that entire pie of happiness, and with it the answer to, "What am I? What is this life, and what is my relationship to it?" This decision allowed me, as I claim, to get the answer to life itself in a matter of only three months. I believe if I can do it, anyone can do it if they have that much "want to."

In that three-month period, all the ailments I had in my physical body corrected. All my miseries dropped away. And I ended up in a place in which I was happy all the time, without sorrow. Not that the world stopped pushing against me, it continued–but I was at a place where I could resolve things almost immediately. Having cleared out the negative fears, all the negative "I cannots," I would focus right on the answer to every problem, and get it very quickly. And so, my whole life turned around from being depressed and sick, to being happy all the time, and being in perfect health all the time.

One of the things that happened in this process was my identification with others. I saw that we are all related, we are all interconnected, each mind is like a radio broadcasting and receiving station; that we are all tuned into each other unconsciously–that we are just not aware of it. As a lot of the suppressed energies are let out, this becomes obvious to us and once we identify with everyone else it is just natural that we want everyone else to discover what we have discovered. That life was meant to be beautiful… meant to be happy all the time with no sorrow. And to be with perfect health. And so after reaching that high point of understanding in 1952, I have wanted to help others to discover what I had discovered.

I was deeply moved by Lester's story because it offered hope for all of us who may not have had the good fortune to have an ideal life. Lester was able to discover his true nature in a relatively short time and despite extreme adversity. If he could do it, I knew that I could, too.

The following quote is Lester expanding more about his actual realization:

I was at the end of my rope. I was told not to take a step unless I absolutely had to because there was a possibility that I could drop dead at any moment.

This was a terrible, shocking thing, suddenly to be told that I couldn't be active anymore, having been so active all my life. It was a horrible thing. An intense fear of dying overwhelmed me, the fear that I might drop dead any minute. This stayed with me for days. I went through a real, horrible, low, spinning period there, in the grip of intense fear of dying or of being a cripple for the rest of my life in that I wouldn't be able to be active. I felt that life would not be worthwhile any more.

This caused me to conclude with determination, "Either I get the answers, or I'll take me off this earth. No heart attack will do it!" I had a nice easy way to do it, too. I had morphine the doctors gave me for my kidney stone attacks.

After several days of this intense fear of dying, I suddenly realized, "Well, I'm still alive. As long as I'm alive there's hope. As long as I'm alive, maybe I can get out of this. What do I do?"

Well, I was always a smart boy, always made the honor roll. Even got myself a four-year scholarship to Rutgers University at a time when scholarships were very rare through competitive examinations. But what does this avail me? Nothing! Here I am with all this brilliance, as miserable and scared as can be.

Then I said, "Lester, you were not only not smart, you were

Dumb! Dumb! Dumb! There's something wrong in your intellect. With all your knowledge, you've come to this bottom end! Drop all this knowledge you've so studiously picked up on philosophy, psychology, social science, and economics! It is of no avail! Start from scratch. Begin all over again your search for the answers.

And with an extreme desperation and intense wanting out–not wanting to die, I began to question, "What am I? What is this world? What is my relationship to it? What do I want from it?"

"Happiness."

"Well, what is happiness?"

"Being loved."

"But I am loved. I know several very desirable girls with beauty, charm, and intellect who want me. And I have the esteem of my friends. Yet, I'm miserable!"

I sensed that the closest thing related to happiness was love. So I began reviewing and reliving my past love affairs, looking at the points where the little happiness that I had were. I began to pull up and dissect all my high moments of loving. Suddenly, I got an inkling that it was when I was loving that I had the highest feeling!

I remembered one evening, a beautiful balmy evening in the mountains when I was camping with my girlfriend. We were both lying on the grass, both looking up at the sky, and I had my arm around her. The nirvana, the perfection of the height of happiness was right there. I was feeling how great is love for my girlfriend! How wonderful is knowing all this nature! How perfect a setting!

Then I saw that it was my loving her that was the cause of this happiness! Not the beauty of the setting or being with my girlfriend.

Then I immediately turned to the other side. Boy it was great when she loved me! I remembered the moment when publicly this beautiful, charming girl told the world that she approved of Lester, she loved Lester–and I could feel that nice feeling of approval. But I sensed that it was not as great as what I had just discovered. It was not a lasting feeling. It was just for the moment. In order for me to have that feeling continuously, she had to continue saying that.

So, this momentary ego approval was not as great as the feeling of loving her! As long as I was loving her, I felt so happy. But when she loved me, there were only moments of happiness when she gave me approval.

Days of further cogitation gradually revealed to me that this was correct! I was happier when I loved her than I was when I got that momentary ego-satisfaction when she loved me. Her loving me was a momentary pleasure that needed constant showing and proving on her part, while my loving her was a constant happiness, as long as I was loving her.

I concluded that my happiness equated to my loving! If I could increase my loving, then I could increase my happiness! This was the first inkling I had as to what brings about happiness. And it was a tremendous thing because I hadn't had happiness. And I said, "Gee, if this is the key to happiness, I've got the greatest!" Even the hope of getting more and more happiness was a tremendous thing, because this was the number one thing I wanted–happiness.

That started me on weeks and weeks of reviewing my past love affairs. I dug up from the past, incident after incident when I thought I was loving, and I discovered that I was being nice to my girlfriends, trying to get them to love me, and that that was selfish. That was not really love. That was just wanting my ego bolstered!

I kept reviewing incidents from the past, and where I saw that I was not loving, I would change that feeling to loving that person.

Instead of wanting them to do something for me, I would change it to my wanting to do something for them. I kept this up until I couldn't find any more incidents to work on.

This insight on love, seeing that happiness was determined by my capacity to love, was a tremendous insight. It began to free me, and any bit of freedom when you're plagued feels so good. I knew that I was in the right direction. I had gotten hold of a link of the chain of happiness and was determined not to let go until I had the entire chain.

I felt a greater freedom. There was an easier concentration of my mind because of it. And I began to look better at my mind. What is my mind? What is intelligence?

Suddenly, a picture flashed of amusement park bumper-cars that are difficult to steer so that they continually bump into each other. They all get their electrical energy from the wire screen above the cars through a pole coming down to every car.

The power above was symbolic of the overall intelligence and energy of the universe coming down the pole to me and everyone else, and to the degree we step on the gas do we use it. Each driver of the cars is taking the amount of energy and intelligence that he wants from that wire, but he steers his car blindly and bumps into other cars, and bumps and bumps.

I saw that if I chose to, I could take more and more of that overall intelligence.

And so I dug into that. I began to examine thinking and its relationship to what was happening. And it was revealed that everything that was happening had a prior thought behind it and that I never before related the thought and the happening because of the element of time between the two.

When I saw that everything that was happening to me had a thought of it before it happened, I realized that if I could grab hold of this, I could consciously determine everything that was happening to me!

And above all, I saw that I was responsible for everything that had happened to me, formerly thinking that the world was abusing me! I saw that my whole past life, and all that tremendous effort to make money and in the end, failing, was due only to my thinking!

This was a tremendous piece of freedom, to think that I was not a victim of this world, that it lay within my power to arrange the world the way I wanted it to be, that rather than being an effect of it, I could now be at cause over it and arrange it the way I would like it to be!

That was a tremendous realization, a tremendous feeling of freedom!

I was so ill when I started my searching; I had one foot in the grave. And when I saw that my thinking was cause for what was happening to me, I immediately saw my body from my chin down to my toes as perfect. And instantly, I knew it was perfect! I knew the lesions and adhesions of my intestine due to perforated ulcers were undone. I knew everything within me was in perfect running order.

And it was.

Discovering that my happiness equated to my loving, discovering that my thinking was the cause of things happening to me in my life gave me more and more freedom. Freedom from unconscious compulsions that I had to work, I had to make money, and I had to have girls. Freedom in the feeling that I was now able to determine my destiny, I was now able to control my world, I was now able to arrange my environment to suit me. This new freedom lightened my internal burden so greatly that I felt that I had no need to do anything.

Plus, the new happiness I was experiencing was so great! I was experiencing a joy that I had never known existed. I had never dreamed happiness could be so great.

I determined "If this is so great, I'm not going to let go of it until I carry it all the way!" I had no idea how joyous a person could be.

So, I began digging further on how to extend this joy. I began further changing my attitudes on love. I would imagine the girl I wanted most marrying one of my friends, or the boy I would want her to marry least, and then enjoy their enjoying each other. To me, this was the extreme in loving, and if I could achieve it, it would give me more of this wonderful thing that I was experiencing.

And so I worked on it. I took a particular fellow, Burl, and a particular girl, and I wouldn't let go until I could really feel the joy of their enjoying each other.

Then I knew I had it–or almost had it.

Then later on, I had further tests of this in talking to people who were opposing me no end when I was trying to help them. I would consciously feel the greatest love for them when they were attacking me. And the joy of loving them was so wonderful, I would, without any thought, thank them so profusely for having given me the opportunity of talking with them, that it threw them into a dither.

But I really felt that. I thanked them from the bottom of my heart for having given me the opportunity of loving them when they were making it as difficult as they possibly could. I didn't express that to them. I just thanked them for the opportunity of having been able to talk with them.

That I was able to do this was good news to me because, like other things, I was able to carry loving to the extreme. I could love people who were opposing me.

And I would not stop until I could see the end of the line of this happiness I was getting. I would go higher and higher and higher and say, "Oh, my gosh, there can be nothing higher than this!" But I would try. And, I would go higher. Then I would say, "Oh, there can't be anything higher than this!" But I would try, and go higher! And then say, "Oh, there can't be anything happier than this!" until I realized there was no limit to happiness!

I would get incapacitated. I could look at my body, and I couldn't move it I was so top-heavy with ecstasy and joy. I was actually incapacitated. I would do this for hours, going higher and higher and then I would have to work for hours to keep coming down and down and down until I could start being the body again in order to operate it.

Contemplating the source of intelligence and energy, I discovered that energy, as well as intelligence was available in unlimited amounts, and that it came simply by my freeing myself from all compulsions, inhibitions, entanglements, hang-ups. I saw that I had dammed up this energy, this power, and all I had to do was pry loose the logs of the dam which were my compulsions and hang-ups—and that was what I did. As I let go of these things, I was removing logs and allowing this infinite energy to flow, just like a water dam flows if you pull the logs out, one by one. The more logs you pull out, the greater the flow. All I needed to do was to remove these logs and let the infinite power and energy flow.

Seeing this, the power that was right behind my mind was allowed to flow through like it had never flowed before. There were times when I'd get this realization of what I am that would put so much energy into me, I would just jump up in the air from my chair. I would go right straight out the front door, and I would start walking and walking and walking, for hours at a time–sometimes for days at a time! I just felt as though my body would not contain it, that I had to walk or run some of it off. I remember walking the streets of New York City in the wee hours of the morning, just walking at a very good pace, and not being able to do anything otherwise! I had to expend some of that energy. It was so tremendous.

I saw that the source of all this energy, of all intelligence was basically harmonious, and that harmony was the rule of the universe. And that was why the planets were not colliding, and that was why the sun rose every day, and that was why everything functioned.

When I started my search, I was a very convinced and absolute materialist. The only thing that was real was that which you could feel and touch. My understanding of the world was as solid as concrete. And when some of these revelations came to me that the world was just a result of my mind, that thinking determined all matter, that matter had no intelligence, and that our intelligence determined all matter and everything about it. When I saw that the solidity that I formerly had was only a thought itself, my nice, solid, concrete foundations began to crack. Twenty years of buildup began to tumble.

And my body shook, and shook so much; I just shook for days. I shook just like a nervous old person. I knew that the concrete view I had had of the world was never going to be again. But it didn't drop away gracefully, with ease. For days, I actually shook, until I think I shook the whole thing loose.

Then, my view was just the opposite of what it had been

months previously, that the real solid thing was not the physical world, was not my mind, but something, that was much greater. The very essence, the very Beingness of me was the reality. It had no limits, it was eternal, and all the things that I saw before were the least of me, rather than the all of me. The all of me was by Beingness.

I saw that the only limitations I had were the ones that I accepted. So, wanting to know what am I? And looking for this unlimited Being that I had had an inkling of, I got insight of this tremendous unlimited Being that I am.

And on seeing that, I right there and then realized, "Well, I'm not this limited body and I thought I was! I am not this mind with its limitations that I thought I was!"

And I undid all body limitation, and almost all mind limitation, just by saying, "I am not it! Finished! Done! Period! That's it!" I so declared.

It was obvious to me that I wasn't that body and mind that I had thought I was. I just saw that's all! It's simple when you see it.

I let go of identifying with this body. And when I did that, I saw that my Beingness was all Beingness. That Beingness is like one grand ocean. It's not chopped up into parts called drops of bodies. It's all one ocean.

This caused me to identify with every being, every person and even every atom in this universe. Then you are finished forever with separation and all the hellishness that's caused only by separation.

Then you can no more be fooled by the apparent limitations of the world. You see them as a dream, as an appearancy, because you know that your very own Beingness has no limits.

In reality, the only thing that is, is Beingness. That is the real, changeless substance behind everything.

Everything of life itself was open to me, the total understanding of it. It is simply that we are infinite beings, over which we have superimposed concepts of limitation (the logs of the dam). And we are smarting under these limitations that we accept for ourselves as though they are real, because they are opposed to our basic nature of total freedom.

Life before and after my realization was at two different extremes. Before, it was just extreme depression, intense misery, and sickness. After, it was a happiness and serenity that's indescribable. Life became so beautiful and so harmonious that all day, every day, everything would fall perfectly into line.

As I would drive through New York City, I would rarely hit a red light. When I would go to park my car, people, sometimes two or three people, would stop and even step into the street to help direct me into a parking space. There were times when taxi cab drivers would see me looking for a parking space and would give up their space for me. And after they did, they couldn't understand why they had done it. There they were, double-parked!

Even policemen who were parked would move out and give me their parking place. And again, after they did, they couldn't understand why. But I knew they felt good in doing so. And they would continue to help me.

If I went into a store, the salesman would happily go out of his way to help me. Or, if I would order something in a restaurant and then change my mind, the waitress would bring what I wanted, even though I hadn't told her.

Actually everyone moves to serve you as you just float around. When you are in tune and you have a thought, every atom in the universe moves to fulfill your thought. And this is true.

Being in harmony is such a delightful, delectable state, not because things are coming your way, but because of the feeling of God-in-operation. It's a tremendous feeling; you just can't imagine how great it is. It is such a delight when you're in tune, in harmony—you see God everywhere! You're watching God in operation. And that is what you enjoy, rather than the time, the incident, the happening. His operation is the ultimate.

When we get in tune, our capacity to love is so extreme that we love everyone with an extreme intensity that makes living the most delightful it could ever be.

When I found the quote above I was deeply moved, and as I worked to put this book together I knew it was important for you to be exposed to it as well so you could appreciate the point of view from which Lester did his teaching.

Lester dedicated the rest of his life, from 1952 through his death in 1994, as he put it, to "helping the rest of him discover what he had discovered." He joyously lived for others without any sense of sacrifice, tirelessly working to help them to discover their true nature or at least let go of their suffering. Despite his best intentions he was not always understood. He used to say, "You only hear ten percent of what I say." Which, in my experience working with him and watching how others related to him, was quite generous. In fact, the very people that he helped the most often vehemently opposed him. But this never deterred him, nor did it ever shake his unqualified happiness and peace.

He worked with people on a one-to-one basis and in small groups, teaching sessions very much like those you will experience in this book. Until, around 1974, with the help of some of his closest students, he summarized his teaching into a do-it-yourself system that we now call the Sedona Method®. He did this to take himself out of the teaching loop. No matter how often he protested to the contrary, his students would often attribute their gains and realizations to him because they felt so elevated in his presence. He wanted everyone to know that they could discover just what he had on their own without needing an external teacher.

As you read this book and work with the material contained with in it, you will have a direct experience of Lester's teaching style through his words and their import. This is significant because it is something that very few people were lucky enough to experience during the last twenty years of his life. You will also have the benefit of seeing how his teachings have evolved since the creation of the Sedona Method® and in the work of his students since his passing.

Before Lester died, he asked me to continue his work and to continue to find ways to make the experience of letting go more readily available to those who are interested. That is why I have added some commentary and suggestions at the end of each session. I hope you will find these as helpful as I did.

I urge you to treat this book as a home study course in discovering your true nature and uncovering your innate happiness. You can benefit from this book even if you only read it casually. But if you dedicate yourself to using it to the fullest, the results you can achieve will astound you.

How to Gain the Maximum Benefit from This Book

A Seven-week Course on Liberating the
Happiness, Peace, and Joy Within

This book is designed to be a seven-week home study course on the ultimate happiness. Read and work with one chapter per week. Each chapter contains a session from Lester along with my comments and suggestions to help you understand his message, as well as space for note and realizations. However, I would suggest that you do your best to get the most out of Lester's words in each session before moving on to the commentary. You may need to allow some extra time to sit with each paragraph or the whole session. You may also want to revisit the chapter repeatedly throughout the week.

You Have All the Time in the World

We live in an incredibly fast paced world where we are constantly forcing ourselves to move more rapidly in order just to keep up. In our rush to attain our goals, especially in the spiritual realm, we are often rushing past the very moment that offers the greatest opportunity for self-recognition—now. If you read this book in a hurry you may find you get what Lester used to call "spiritual indigestion." Therefore, I highly encourage you to read this material and approach it as an exploration of life as though you have all the time in the world.

Don't Believe Anything We Say

Especially with spiritual teachers, there is a tendency simply to accept what they say on hearsay or belief. Lester strongly felt that we should avoid doing this with any teacher. Instead we should allow ourselves to stay open to a teacher's message as an exploration or an experiment in consciousness. We should only accept what he or she teaches once we can prove it for ourselves through our own experience. Lester used to call this "taking it for checking."

I suggest that you take everything that you are exposed to in this book for checking. Allow yourself to be as open to the message as you can without accepting it on blind faith. You will find that this material has much more value for you when you explore it in your own life.

On the other hand, I also highly recommend that you suspend comparison and judgment as best you can. You may find that some of what you are exposed to in this book contradicts what you have learned from other teachers. I would suggest that you do not throw out the other material that you have learned, but merely put it aside as best you can while you explore these sessions. Once you have had time to draw your own conclusions, then you can go back and compare this material to everything else you have learned and see where it fits.

Contradiction is inevitable when you compare different paths or traditions of growth. However, this does not invalidate the different points of view. What every good teacher does is speak to the audience at hand to the best of their ability. Sometimes they may appear to contradict themselves because each audience they address needs to experience the teachings from different levels or perspectives. For this reason you may even notice apparent contradictions between me and Lester and Lester and himself. Contradiction can be most palpable when you compare different teachers. Not only are they speaking to different audiences, they are also bringing their own unique perspective to the topic–as they should be.

When it comes to truth, if you can allow yourself to embrace all possibilities you will find yourself understanding and applying the wisdom you gain on a much more useful, deeper, and heartfelt level. There are many rays that lead to the one sun.

It Is a Matter of Resonance

From my perspective, everything in the world has its own vibration or resonance, including you and everyone you meet. Have you ever noticed that some people tend to pull you up when you are with them and others seem to pull you down, and that they often don't need to say or do anything to have this effect on you? As we grow in understanding on the path, our resonance or frequency tends to go up. But it is not just a matter of higher or lower. We all relate better with some people than others, even if they are on the same level of vibration as us. Of course the same thing is true for teachers.

As you read this material, you may find that you resonate intensely with certain statements while others leave you feeling blank or unmoved. Lester recommended that you highlight the chapters, phrases, or statements that move you most for future reference, then go back and spend some time pondering them. Over time, as you revisit this material, other parts of it will stand out more than they did initially. That is because you will have changed and become ready to see things from a new perspective. When this happens, allow yourself to honor the change and shift your focus accordingly.

About Lester's Language

Lester had a unique way of using the English language. I have purposely preserved his style of communication because I've noticed that when you read or listen to any teacher in his or her own vernacular, the words have more of an import than when they have been heavily edited. My intention here is to give you the feel of having been present as Lester's talks unfolded, so that you can be as open as possible to his deepest message.

Lester came to this unique communication style for several reasons. His realization came quickly and spontaneously without him following any particular teacher or discipline or even having done any reading or studying of the path. Thus he had no language that adequately expressed what he was experiencing and what he wanted to share with others. As a result he looked in existing spiritual books from both the East and the West to try and find a suitable language that would best communicate his amazing discoveries. From the East, he was attracted to the teachings and writings of Ramana Maharshi and Paramahansa Yogananda. From the West, he drew upon the Bible, especially the New Testament. You will probably notice the influence of these sources in his writing. Occasionally he even slips into old English to express himself.

Most of the Lester material in this book comes from talks that took place in the 1960's and early 1970's. Therefore he often uses a vernacular that was more appropriate for that era. You will notice that his reference to current events and things like population figures are also reflective of that same time period.

In addition, Lester had difficulty grounding himself in time. He saw time as a self-imposed limitation or merely a concept. He would refer to things as happening yesterday that happened ten or twenty years earlier, and things that were about to happen that have yet to occur. He always seemed to be factually accurate and yet frequently was not able to place his perceptions in the appropriate time period.

Lester also did not believe in the limitation of space, so here and there often had the same meaning to him. He would often refer to getting "there" when referring to Beingness when he really meant "here." Or "going free" when he knew there was nowhere to go. He also used language this way because he was wanting to communicate to people where they were. Most people believe that Beingness is apart from where they are now. That's why they go looking for it. The "there" that Lester referred to when speaking of Beingness is closer than your breath.

Lester also learned his instructing style from an old school that uses imperatives heavily. He often used the charged words "should," "have to," "must," and "only." These charged words were often used by Lester to wake people up by using a little extra force. If you notice that these words stir up resistance in you, this in normal. These words tend to do that in most of us. Allow yourself to let go of the resistance as best you can and be open to the underlying message.

Please keep these points in mind as you read the sessions so you can allow yourself to remain as open as possible to his message without getting lost in how it is being communicated.

When Two or More Are Gathered in Thy Name

The exercises that follow each session have been or will be explored as part of the advanced courses we teach at Sedona Training Associates. They are designed so that you can benefit from either doing them on your own or sharing them with a friend, relative, or loved one. There is an awesome power that is unleashed when we gather together to focus on truth. That is why Sedona Training Associates hosts live seminars to explore this topic and why you can benefit from sharing this material with others.

If you choose to do the exercises at the end of each session with someone else, you can ask each other the questions or lead each other in the explorations. All you need to do is be as present as you can with your partner and ask them the questions in the third person using the pronoun "you" instead of "I." Grant your partner their Beingness by allowing them to have their own exploration.

When you are asking your partner to let go, do your best to let go as you facilitate your partner in releasing. You will find that this happens naturally if you are open to it. Refrain from leading, judging their responses, or giving them advice. Also refrain from discussing the explorations until you have both completed them during that sitting and you mutually agree to discuss them. Also validate your partner's point of view even if it does not agree with your own.

Please refrain from playing the role of counselor or therapist unless you're a trained counselor or therapist and have been specifically asked by your partner to play this role with them. Also, if they bring up a medical condition that would ordinarily require a trained medical professional, suggest that they get whatever support they need in this area. If you are not sure whether or not they truly need medical support, you can suggest it anyhow, just to be sure.

Write Down Your Gains

As you move diligently through this material, you will find that it has many powerful positive effects on you. We call the changes that come from this exploration "gains," and I highly recommend that you write them down, as they occur, to spur you on to even greater self-discovery.

The following is a list of some gains you can expect as you work with this book:

- Positive changes in behavior and/or attitude
- Greater ease, effectiveness, and joy in daily activities
- More open and effective communications
- Increased problem solving ability
- Greater flexibility
- More relaxed and confident in action
- Accomplishments
- Completions
- New beginnings
- Acquiring new abilities or skills
- Increase in positive feelings
- Decrease in negative feelings
- More love towards all beings

As you read and explore this material you will also have realizations about your own patterns of limitation and realizations about the nature of Reality itself. I highly recommend that you write these down as well.

There are seven blank pages at the end of each session, one for each day of the week, which are designed for you to write down your gains and realizations.

Be Open to the Unexpected

Realizations and gains definitely will come as you consciously work with this material, however, they will also come when you least expect them. Often it is when we are not looking for, or trying to accomplish anything that the mind relaxes enough to allow realization. So make room for this possibility throughout your day. As best you can, relax and accept that the timing of your greatest breakthroughs and realizations, including the ultimate realization of your true nature, may be totally out of your control.

It Is All a Matter of Letting Go or Releasing

Lester strongly believed that growing on the path was a function of your willingness, ability, and follow-through in letting go. He was so adamant about this point that he dedicated the last twenty years of his life solely to this one aspect of his teachings and encouraged the development and practice of what we now call the Sedona Method®. To get the most from this book, I highly recommend that you learn the Sedona Method® and practice it as you read and work with Lester's material. Even if you don't, I highly encourage you to do some form of letting go in order to deal with whatever this material invariably brings up into your consciousness.

You will get the most out of it if you allow yourself to let go as best you can.

To this end, I will be making suggestions throughout the book of what and how to let go as you explore what Lester has to offer. I have also included the following guidelines on releasing so that you can start to apply this technique in your life as you study this course in the ultimate happiness.

Holistic Releasing™

Holistic Releasing™ is the latest advancement in the continuing improvement and development of the process that we at Sedona Training Associates call letting go, releasing, or the Sedona Method®. If you've worked with us before, you're aware that in our Sedona Method® classes and taped programs we mainly focus on three methods of letting go. The first is letting go by choosing or making a decision just to drop whatever we're holding onto in the present moment. The second is letting go by allowing whatever is to be in this moment, welcoming it fully and seeing it almost like the clouds that pass through the sky, needing no correction, no changing, no fixing. The third way is letting go by diving into the very core of whatever the feeling is. When we dive into the very core of any feeling, we discover that it's empty inside–or full of goodness–not full of the darkness that we generally assume will be there.

I recently developed a fourth way of letting go that we call Holistic Releasing™. This process is what many of the suggestions at the end of each chapter are all about. It has two purposes. If you've worked with the Sedona Method® before, it's a way of deepening the work that you're already doing. And if you haven't worked with the Sedona Method® before, it's a way to open your understanding of the whole process of letting go. It is a way of having whatever you want in life.

The Holistic Releasing™ process will help you to collapse, dissolve, or let go of whatever sense of inner limitation you may be experiencing in your life. As you work with the suggestions throughout this book, your understanding of this new process will deepen and you'll find yourself spontaneously practicing this process in life–noticing more possibilities and seeing alternatives. You will feel more flexible, more open, and much more capable of handling whatever life dishes out to you.

Holistic Releasing™ is based on the premise that everything we experience in life, whether real or imagined, arises in pairs or polarities or duality. Because of life's underlying unity, if we have "in," we also have "out." If we have "right," we also have "wrong." If we have "good," we also have "bad." If we have "pain," we also have pleasure." This is quite obvious. However when we live life as though we can hold onto the good and get rid of the bad, we miss the inner truth. When we try to hold onto something good, it always slips away. Whenever we try to clutch onto what we judge as good or preferable, it tends to move through our awareness.

Then think about the converse. What happens when we resist or try to hold away what we don't like? That is right. It persists or gets even bigger. So in effect what we've been doing is pulling what we don't like towards us and pushing what we do like away. We also spend a lot of time and energy magnifying the polarity by trying to keep what we like as far away as possible from what we don't like. All of this is creating the exact opposite effect of what we want: magnifying or even creating what we call problems.

I have discovered that when you bring the two sides of a

polarity together, it's like bringing matter and antimatter together, or positive and negative energy. The pair neutralizes each other and you're left with much greater freedom, greater presence, and greater understanding. You see solutions, not problems. You feel more open, more alive, and more at peace. As you work with the material in this book, you'll discover that this effect magnifies over time. You will start to discover more possibilities and see things more clearly. Every time you work with any of the suggestions in this book, you'll get more out of them—more inner understanding.

Now, the way we do this is very simple. We simply focus on both sides of the polarity by going back and forth. For instance, a very simple polarity has to do with happiness. Most of us are either feeling relatively happy or unhappy from moment to moment, and we see only one, not the other. So let's just do a little experiment. Could you allow yourself to feel as unhappy as you do in this moment? And then, could you allow yourself to feel as happy as you do in this moment? And as unhappy as you do in this moment? And as happy as you do in this moment? Do this a few more times and then notice how you feel inside.

To practice Holistic Releasing™, I suggest you continually go back and forth on each side of the particular polarity you are exploring. Do this several times in a row and you'll notice something happening inside. The polarities dissolve each other. You may have already noticed this just by doing the exercise. You are left with greater and greater freedom and presence. You may see the underlying unity beneath the apparent duality and separation of the polarities. You may also experience it as an energetic shift. You may feel it as a sense of dissolving or clearing or lightness. You may have greater clarity and understanding within your own self.

The way to get the most out of this process is merely to stay as open and as fully engaged as you can from moment to moment. As you ask the questions or repeat the statements to yourself, please do so with as open a mind and a heart as possible, doing your best not to lead with either one. If you must lead with one, do your best to lead with your heart–your feeling sense. Allow yourself to be as open as you can to the thoughts, feelings, sensations, and pictures that arise when you repeatedly ponder the statements or questions. Even better, try not to do anything except to stay open on every level. Let this process–releasing–do you.

The initial results from working with a polarity may be subtle. But as you work with it, the results will become more and more profound. And if you're persistent in working on any particular polarity, you'll reach a place of neutrality, or you'll reach a place of great expansion inside, as you've dissolved your sense of limitation.

You may reach a point where you feel as though you've had enough. If this does happen, you can either allow yourself to relax even more into the process or simply take a break. Do something to break the pattern of the moment. Go for a walk, stand up and stretch, open your eyes and look around the room, or close your eyes if you had them open. Then come back to working with yourself.

Do your best to start noticing how you create artificial polarities in life and begin to bring the two sides of these polarities together. Even in noticing them they will start to dissolve, leaving you with growing understanding and freedom. Please let yourself enjoy this work that we do together. Allow it to be fun and easy. Remember, growth can be fun!

The following questions and answers will help you get the

most from the process of releasing. In addition to reading them now, review them as often as needed as you work through the material in this book.

How can I best do this process?

This process will help you to free yourself from all of your unwanted patterns of behavior, thought, and feeling. All that it requires from you is to be as open as you can to the process. It will free you to access clearer thinking, yet it is not a thinking process. It will help you to access heightened creativity, although you don't need to be particularly creative to be effective at doing this.

Sometimes we will use statements and sometimes we will use questions. When we use questions, we are merely asking you if it is possible to take this action. "Yes" or "No" are both acceptable answers. You will often let go even if you say, "No." As best you can, answer the question that you choose with a minimum of thought, staying away from second-guessing or getting into a debate with yourself about the merits of this action or its consequences. All the questions used in this process are deliberately simple. They are not important in and of themselves, but rather are designed to point you to the experience of letting go.

This process actually does itself. By simply switching back and forth in your mind between the two unique points of view that make up each polarity, they dissolve each other. As you work with this material, simply be as engaged as you can with an open mind and heart. Allow whatever thoughts, feelings, and limiting beliefs or pictures arise in your consciousness to just be there–welcome them as fully as you can. You do not even need to try and let them go. They will naturally dissolve each other.

What are some of the ways I can apply this in my life?

Any time you find yourself being able to perceive only one possibility, either internally or externally, there is a high likelihood that you are missing at least one or more possibilities. Develop the habit of looking for alternatives and then doing the releasing process to gain more inner clarity.

If you find yourself judging yourself or others, you can simply allow yourself to switch back and forth between the judgment you have and its opposite. If you find yourself stuck in any way, allow yourself to be as stuck as you are and as unstuck as you are. Allow yourself to be creative as you work with this process, and you will find yourself seeing more and more possibilities and opening to having it all including the ultimate happiness.

The following is a list of generic questions that you can use to work on your own issues and polarities:

Could I allow myself to resist _____ as much as I do?
Could I allow myself to welcome (allow) _____ as best as I can?

Could I allow myself to reject _____ as much as I do?
Could I allow myself to accept _____ as best as I can?

Could I allow myself to dislike _____ as much as I do?
Could I allow myself to like _____ as much as I do?

Could I allow myself to hate _____ as much as I do?
Could I allow myself to love _____ as best as I can?

Could I allow myself to want to change _____ as much as I do?
Could I allow myself to let go of wanting to change _____ as best I can?

Could I allow myself to say no to _____ ?

Could I allow myself to say yes to _____ ?

Could I allow myself to be as open to _____ as I am?
Could I allow myself to be as closed to _____ as I am?

What does it feel like to release?

The experience of releasing can widely vary depending on the individual. Most people feel an immediate sense of lightness or relaxation as they use the process. Others feel energy moving in their bodies as though they are coming back to life. You will also notice that your mind gets progressively quieter and your remaining thoughts clearer. You will start to see more solutions rather than just problems. Over time it may even feel positively blissful. The changes become more pronounced the longer you practice.

How do I know I'm doing it right?

If you notice any positive shifts in feeling, attitude, or behavior, then you are doing it right. However, every issue you work on may require different amounts of releasing. If at first it doesn't shift completely, release and release again. Continue releasing until you have achieved your desired result.

What if I feel I don't know how to release?

We were all born with the innate ability to let go. If you have ever watched a happy baby you know what I mean. Because this ability was not under our conscious control, over time we forgot how to do it. However, it is so natural that it doesn't require thinking, just as we don't think, "breathe," every time we take a breath.

Another way to look at it is with the example of a light

switch. The first time you turned a light switch did you know how it worked? Probably not. Nevertheless, the light turned on and you were able to experience the benefit of the light right away, before you ever understood how it operated.

The more you can lead with your heart and not your mind in this process, the easier it is to do. If you find you are getting stuck in wanting to figure it out, try letting go of the wanting to figure it out, and see what happens.

How could something this simple be so powerful?

The most powerful and usable things in life are often the simplest. When things are allowed to remain simple, they are easy to remember and duplicate.

No one has to convince you how critically important breathing is, yet if I were to give you a procedure to follow for breathing it would be: "Breathe in–breathe out. Repeat as needed." What could be simpler? Yet there is little that is more fundamental to your life. As you use Holistic Releasing™ over time, you will discover that it can become as easy as second nature and require as little thought as breathing does now.

What should I do if I find myself getting caught up into old patterns of behavior or I just plain forget to release?

First, it is important to remember that this is to be expected and it's OK. Your ability to release will increase over time. When you recognize that there is a problem, you can always release now.

When learning to release, you may go through the following progression:

1. You will do things just the way you did them before and you will only remember to release afterwards. The moment you recognize

that there is a problem, simply release.

2. Over time, you will start to catch yourself in the middle, when you are involved in the old behavior pattern. You can release when you recognize that you are doing it again, and you will find that you are able to change the old pattern.

3. Over more time, you will catch yourself about to get caught up in the pattern again and you will release and not do it.

4. Finally, you won't even need to release about that particular tendency because you will have completely let it go.

If you allow yourself to be persistent, your attitude and effectiveness will eventually change for the better, even about long-standing problems. It is also helpful to schedule short releasing breaks throughout your day to remind yourself to release.

Relax, Have Fun, and Enjoy

As you work through the book, you may find your life getting lighter and freer and more alive. You may also find that you start to uncover some of the universal truths for which you have been striving. Congratulations on beginning this journey to the place that you have never left–the heart of awareness. It is my sincerest hope that this material will quickly help you to discover and live a life filled with a happiness without sorrow, a joy without bounds, and a peace and bliss that surpass all understanding.

"If you could let go of thinking, and in just one easy thought with no other thoughts around think, 'I am perfect,' you'd instantly have a perfect body."

Lester Levenson

Session 1

A Perfect Body

Should we try to achieve a perfect body? I would say yes, definitely yes, if you can't do it.

Q: If you cannot do it?

Lester: Yes.

Q: That's a contradiction!

Lester: No. Change your inability to being able. If you cannot perfect the body, you should learn to do so.

Although we should be able to perfect the body, once we are able to do that, then it is better to let the body be the way it is, healthy or sick, and not be affected by it. When one has enough understanding, no matter what happens to the body, it is all the same to him. I've given you an over-all approach, and now I'll go into it in more detail.

If we want a perfect body, and we don't have a perfect body, it means that we don't have the conviction that we can make the body perfect. It means we are subconsciously holding in our mind a consciousness of an imperfect body. The body is an exact copy of the mind, the body being only our consciousness projected outwardly. We must change our subconscious thinking until we subconsciously have the conviction that our body is perfect. That will do it.

Now, is it necessary to have a perfect body? No, it is not. However, it is necessary to have a perfect understanding. To get this understanding, if you cannot have a perfect body, then learn to make your body perfect. When you can, then go beyond the necessity of a perfect body by getting the spiritual understanding of "I am not the body" and "The body does not affect me." This is a much higher state. In fact, this is one of the highest of states: to be able to maintain your equanimity regardless of what is happening to the body!

This body is not infinite. It's an extremely limited vehicle and is very, very delicate. Change the internal temperature twelve degrees and it dies. Put tiny amounts of chemicals (poisons) into it and it dies. Cut out oxygen and it dies. So, this body is an extremely limited vehicle. It is much better not to be the physical body, but to be what you really are and get out from under the fear of death, the basic fear behind all other fears.

The discipline of having an imperfect body and not allowing it to bother you is a very high spiritual discipline. Many fully-realized Masters go through life with a sick body, setting an example of non-emphasis on the body, because the body is a cage of limitation. We are not in the body, the body is in us. Our greatest limitation is, "I am this body." Not only is the body a limitation, but also associated with it are hundreds of other limitations.

So, although at first I corrected bodily imperfections instantly, I now prefer not to correct the body, but to have it touch me not–not even in the slightest–regardless of what is happening to it. This is something I started three or four years ago. I can tell you what happens when you do not identify with the body. I was just thinking of the time I was loading trees for firewood onto a truck, and one tree wouldn't go. I said, "I'll make this go," and I gave a tremendous push while I had my shoulder against a tree trunk. The tree went on, and I slipped a disc at the bottom of my spine.

The reason why I mention this incident is that it was an excruciatingly painful one. Immediately, I almost collapsed from the pain. Then I said, "Lester, be not the body." Now what happens is that the body doesn't bother me if I'm not the body. I was aware that there was a pain, but it was like a weak, distant pain, and it did not bother me. I could immediately load other trees. The body acted just as though it were not imperfect.

I've done that at other times. I once sprained an ankle and it swelled. That's painful, too, and when I did not identify with the body, I walked off as though the foot were perfect, yet there was a sprained ankle there. When I had that slipped disc, I'd awaken in the morning and, forgetting, I would not immediately not be the body, and the pain would be severe. To get out of bed, I'd actually have to fall out on my hands and knees. I remember doing this the first day or two. Then I'd shake my head and say, "Wow, what is this?" Recognizing the situation, I would say, "Oh, I am not the body"; then I'd stand up, move through the day as though the body were okay, and the body could do anything and everything. There was a weak, distant pain that I knew was there, but it didn't bother me. Now, this type of disciplining is excellent if one can do it. Be not the body!

Q: Wouldn't it be so much simpler to say, "The body's perfect," and then have a perfect body? After all, you control your body–why even have the pain or feel uncomfortable when you get out of bed?

Lester: Well, when I got out of bed, I was identifying with the body; that's why it pained so. But the moment I didn't, everything was all right. I'd stand up, and the body would do anything. Now, this is a test of your spiritual knowingness. This is much higher. This is being not the body.

Q: How can the body be imperfect when you said before that your body is a reflection of your mentality? And, if you know that there's only perfection, how can you have an imperfect body?

Lester: At first I identified with the body and then, after minutes, I did not. You want me to come down a step? Or do you want me to stay where I am?

Q: All right, go ahead and stay up where you are.

Lester: A perfect body is not the highest state. A body is a limitation even when it's perfect. It's a perfect body. It's still a body, but it's perfect. A higher state is not being the body but being the All. Ah, you're shaking your head now. Have I answered it?

Q: I'm beginning to follow what you're getting at.

Lester: So, again, it's a matter of level, but because we're now into a level that is high, I want to stay there. Be not the body! Be what you really are! Be Infinite! Be the All! Perfection is not a perfect body. Perfection is absolute perfection.

Although you have a tendency to bring it down into perfect things, perfection does not relate to things. No thing is perfect. Everything is a thing of limitation, confined to form and space. So, the top state, the absolute, is a state of no things. It's just Beingness, or pure consciousness, pure awareness. That's not being a body, a thing. It's just Being.

So to sum it up, of course we should have perfect bodies! If we have bodies that pull on our attention all the time, it's difficult to seek the truth. So, rid yourself of bodily demands. Make the body as perfect as you can. However, it is a higher state when the body does not affect us because of our not identifying with the body. Is it clear now, these two different aspects of body? It's great to make a perfect body. It is far better to be not the body.

Q: You see, it's very difficult for me to be Beingness or awareness without being something or aware of something.

Lester: You and most of us. But the top state is just Beingness, only Beingness, or consciousness, only consciousness. It's consciousness conscious of all consciousness. It's Beingness being all Beingness. And consciousness and Beingness mean the same thing at the top.

Q: Well, can't we enjoy the limitation at the time?

Lester: You can. You can if you choose, but that's not the ultimate joy. If you want more joy, don't enjoy the thing–be joy! Happiness is our natural, inherent state. We are the All. We artificially create a lack and then a desire to relieve that lack, which, when that lack is undone, we feel better.

It's like sticking a pin into yourself. It hurts, and you take it out and say, "Gee, that feels good." This is exactly what enjoying things and people is. We hurt ourselves by creating a lack and then remove the lack, the pain, and say, "Gee, that feels good. That makes me happy." Every time you feel happiness, you feel only your real Self, more or less. The happier you are, the more you feel your real Self, and you wrongly attribute it to things and people outside of yourself.

The mechanism of it is this: When you create the lack, you start up thoughts of I need this person, this thing, to make me happy. That causes a bit of pain–a need, a lack–which, when you are relieved of that thought of lack, you return back to being your Self, and this is what we call happiness. This is something very great to be achieved: to see that your happiness is inherent. That which you have been calling happiness is doing away with happiness, and then restoring it and wrongly attributing it to external people and things.

So, if you want to enjoy a body, that's your privilege. If you want more joy, don't enjoy the body, just be joy, which you naturally are. That's the natural state. It's not necessary to need things. When you see that you are the All, there's nothing lacking. So, take your joy directly, be your Self. That's being Infinite joy.

Q: Now step down and discuss your experiences of changing your body, because, really, many of us are in the area where we don't quite understand this. Let's talk about myself, not "we."

Lester: Okay. What happened to me was that I saw that there's as much life in this body as there is in a piece of wood. It's composed of carbohydrates and minerals, the same chemicals as in a piece of wood; the only life in this body is "I." I put the life into the body. I saw that the body is my consciousness, and my consciousness puts the life into it. When you see that you make the body, then you can change it. You can mentally change it.

Now, the body we have now is the accumulated education, body-wise, that we have gathered up-to-date. This is my concept of a body, that's your concept of your body. It's deeply subconscious right now. This is why it's difficult to change the body. To perfect it requires a seemingly impossible letting go of all these past concepts of imperfection of the body. This, however, is the negative way of doing it–that is, of eliminating the negative concepts of imperfection. It's a difficult way.

Then there is the better way, the positive way, of putting in what should be there: a picture of a perfect body in your mind. Now, this picture of the perfect body must be put in with a will power more powerful than the sum total of all the pictures in the past of an imperfect body. You must image the picture of a perfect body with a thought that's stronger than all the past thoughts. Does that make sense? This is the mechanics of it.

All right, now what is a powerful thought? A powerful thought is a concentrated thought. The more concentrated, the more powerful the thought. A concentrated thought is a thought without other extraneous thoughts present at the time. The very best way to get a most powerful thought is to let go of your self, your little self. Let go of your feeling: I am this person, I have this, I have that. Then say, "Yes, there is only perfection, and that includes this body." Let go of the world, let go of your thinking that your mind is your biggest obstacle.

Your mind is going all the time, whether you're aware of it or not. When you're not conscious of it, it's going on subconsciously. You've trained yourself to think, think, think. You've got the mind spinning with all these thoughts. You've given a lot of importance to this thinking. The importance of it is also subconscious, so it's not easy to let go of the importance of thinking. And this is an obstacle to your concentrating.

If you could let go of thinking, and in just one easy thought with no other thoughts around, think "I am perfect," you'd instantly have a perfect body. It'll take a continuous trying until you achieve it. An almost effortless thought is the way it is effected, because your mind is quiet at the time. And you might not even be aware of it when it happens. You might become aware of it later on.

I was just reminded of a case of a man who was in a wheelchair for many years, I believe ten. His house caught on fire, and he packed two bags, ran out of the house and sat down on them. It was after he had sat down on the bags that he had realized what he had done. He had forgotten that he couldn't walk. See, when it does happen, you're accepting the positive so much that the negative is forgotten for the time being.

To sum it up, the thing that will effect a perfect body is a very strong conviction that, "My body is perfect." Saying it another way, it is a concentrated thought, which is a thought undisturbed by other thoughts at the time. And the feeling is a feeling of let go. You just let go and let the perfection be.

Q: Well then, what you're really saying is that when you see all-perfection, your thoughts are so based upon perfection, your body automatically takes that perfection.

Lester: Yes, if you see the all-perfection, then everything is absolutely perfect—everything.

Q: Then you cannot have an imperfect body.

Lester: Right.

Q: And this being very, very peaceful. If you go into psychosomatic medicine, they claim that the body difficulties are caused by turmoil in the mind. And if these are quieted, then the body may be corrected without any thought about it.

Lester: Yes, if you quiet the subconscious mind. You see, the body is working on automatic pilot. Everything happening in the body, we are doing subconsciously, automatically. So, you have to straighten out the subconscious thinking.

Q: When you were in New York and you accomplished much, did you do it systematically? Did you just see perfection so completely, or did you realize the power of your mind? Just exactly what method did you use?

Lester: Well, when I did it, it was almost like a by-product. I sat down with a determination to get the answers to, "Who am I? What am I? What is this world? What is my relationship to it?"

In the process of which, I saw the perfection, and that this universe–including this body–was a product of my consciousness, my thinking. I therefore imaged the body as perfect, and instantly it was. Gone were the ulcers, the jaundice, the coronary trouble and other imperfections. It was very easy. It was like an almost effortless thought.

There are different levels of healing the body. Spiritually, it's instantaneous. There's only perfection, and that's all there is, and it is instantaneous. Mentally, it is done from instantaneously to very fast, in days or in weeks, depending upon your mental concept of how fast you can do it.

Q: When you're using the word "body," it also would include all our environment, wouldn't it? There's really no difference between our body and our environment.

Lester: That's true in the sense that it is all our consciousness, but I'm speaking specifically of the body, because we're talking on that. Actually, the whole material world and the body are very similar in creation. They are the physical out-projecting of our mind.

Have I answered all your questions on it? See, it does not help you much when I tell you what I did. You've got to do it your way. And, as I see it, your way is overcoming the accumulated wrong body-thinking of the past.

Now, this is a carry-over from a prior life. This is how deeply engrained it is in you. If you can perfect it, good. If you can't, don't make a big issue of it, because it's better to live with it and not be it. Get your spiritual understanding. That's far more important. What's so great about the best of bodies? They decay sooner or later. The very best of bodies becomes awfully stenchy sooner or later when it starts decaying. So what's this big thing about bodies? Approach it from a higher point.

Q: As I understand it, if I have a sense of perfection, which would include my body, the body could not be imperfect.

Lester: That's correct. Get it! And when you get it, not only the body, but everything becomes perfect, which is far better than having just a perfect body. Then you have the whole universe perfect, and that's a very, very high state. To see the perfection where the imperfection seems to be is the highest state.

Comments:

If you believe that you can't have a perfect body, then allow yourself to let go until you can have the perfect body. Once you have achieved that, allow yourself to move above it to the state where there is knowingness that you are not the body. The body is the least of you, not the all of you. You would find this easy to do if you did not see the body as real but accepted it as an out-picturing of mind. As Lester used to say, this is either easy or impossible. It can be easy when you truly let go. It is up to you.

Remember, nothing we do in this book is meant to take the place of competent medical attention. We make no claims to treat, diagnose, or cure any disease.

Suggestions for the week:

You can allow yourself to see the perfection of the body if you also allow yourself to welcome and release the apparent imperfection. This simple exercise will help you do so. Focus on your body or on a specific physical problem that you believe you have and then use these questions to allow yourself to dissolve the picture of imperfection. First, "Could I allow my body to appear as imperfect as it does?" Welcome this picture knowing it is just a picture, as best you can. Then, without having to have a conscious picture of perfection, ask yourself "Could I allow the body to be as perfect as it is?"

If you do this exercise with an open mind and heart, and you accept at least the possibility that your body is just a picture in mind, you will find yourself dropping the pictures of an imperfect body and accepting the possibility of perfection here and now.

This next exercise will help you to start to recognize the body as a picture in mind. As you move through life, use these questions to stretch your consciousness beyond the obvious. Allow the body to be in motion, doing whatever it is doing, and then ask yourself: "Am I moving or have I never moved?" Another way to do this is to ask yourself: "I am moving?" Allow yourself to feel, hear, and see what that perception is like. Then ask yourself: "Have I never moved?" Again, allow yourself to perceive what this is like as best you can. Go back and forth between these two perspectives and allow them to dissolve each other. You can take time out to do this exercise or simply occasionally do it throughout your day to interrupt the pattern of believing in the reality of the body.

You can also allow yourself to explore the following polarities:
- I am in the body–The body is in me.
- The body is me–I have never been a body.
- That body has problems–That body is perfect.
- There is a body–There is no body.

The next seven pages of this book are designed to help further your own exploration. You can view them as your diary of progress during the week that you are working with this session. Use the space allowed on each page to write down your gains and realizations as they happen, as well as for notes on working with the various exercises.

Day One

Day Two

Day Three

Day Four

Day Five

Day Six

Day Seven

"Discover who the sufferer is and on
discovering this you will find all joy."

Lester Levenson

Session 2

Growth Can Be Every Day

Most of you don't realize that every day you are presented with wonderful opportunities to make major steps in your growth. Were you to look at and see this, the goal that seems so difficult and elusive would soon be in your possession. Awaken to this fact and be done with worldly miseries.

To do this, you must accept the worldly happenings as they relate to you as your means of growth–yes, even as your teacher. You must look at all the unpleasantries; you must face them squarely with an objective eye, and you must seek and find their cause.

The method should be either or both of two approaches. Whenever someone or something bothers you and you are unhappy, or whenever you react to someone or something, ask yourself, "How and wherein did I cause this?" Look within your mind to find the past thought, now subconscious, that caused the event. Discover the originating thought in you, and you discover your mastership over the event.

The second approach is more readily available to you. Every

time you react or experience something unpleasant, it is always because of some ego-motivation. Ask yourself, "What is my ego (selfish) motivation behind this? What, in this situation, do I want to be different from what it is?" When you discover it, drop it and be freer. Use your daily unpleasantries for growing freer every day. The more you do this, the faster and easier it is to do.

Either or both of the above methods will free you and return to you your mastership in a relatively short time. Make it a habit of using both, or one or the other, every day.

Whenever you're unhappy, do not look for escape from it via distraction, doing something else, or seeking entertainment. This is the worst thing you can do. You will never be able to let go of or eliminate unhappiness. Either discover your mastership of the event or see the ego-motivation behind the misery, and there-by undo that particular unhappiness.

Almost everyone, when unhappy, looks for escape and calls the escape or relief from the misery happiness. This allows the unhappiness pattern to continue in the future. It postpones the time indefinitely as to when one will have to eliminate the unhappiness. Escape is the worst palliative in the world–worse than drugs. Every escape is a complete waste of time and a further continuing and holding onto misery. The more you feel misery, the deeper it becomes ingrained. Therefore, one should not escape from nor remain in misery, but should use one of the above two methods to get out of it permanently.

The Rest of this session is comprised of a series of aphorisms collected from many different talks. Please allow yourself to read them one at a time taking as much time as necessary to uncover their deepest import for you.

- All unhappiness is caused by our trying to be limited, to be an ego. The more we are our Self, the happier we are. We will never be completely happy until we are completely being our Self.

- Why waste time in entertainment, in escape? Looking to entertainment each time delays and pushes the goal a bit further away. Only a realized non-attached Being can enjoy things in the world without creating bondages and miseries.

- What everyone is looking for in entertainment is escape from misery and the happiness of the Self.

- Escaping misery keeps you forever miserable.

- Problems are a constant reminder that we are in the wrong direction.

- Every pain is basically a pain of limiting your Self.

- A person cannot be happy if he has inner anxieties. Anxieties are expecting to happen that which you do not want to happen. Expect only that which you do want.

- It's the ego-sense of being a separate individual that is the source of all trouble.

- All unhappiness is separation. Limitation and misery are the same.

- Misery is caused when an infinite Being tries to be a limited being.

- If, when you are miserable, you would think and feel the opposite, that is what you would effect.

- Misery is complexity. Happiness is simplicity.

- If you see misery, it's your misery. When you see the perfection where the seeming imperfection seems to be, the misery is only an apparency.

- The more miserable you get, the less you should look for an escape (socializing, entertainment). Rather, isolate until you see and let go of the reason for it, or move into your real Self. Never let go of–through escape from misery–a good opportunity to grow.

- Misery is just the whip we set up to whip ourselves into happiness.

- The more we move away from our Self, the more miserable we become, until finally we get so miserable that we cannot take it anymore, and then we begin to move back into our Self.

- You create a lie when you say, "I don't have," and that starts the unhappiness of not having.

- Any time you're miserable, you're dwelling in your ego. Just being miserable should be a realigner for you. Say, "Here, I am in the wrong direction," then change it, and you'll be happy again.

- Anyone can feel happy; anyone can feel miserable. You don't have to see why–just change it!

- Every worldly attachment is a dedication to misery.

- Misery is the setting up of limitation.

- Misery is to the degree that we think we are limited.

- Every pleasure in the world has an accompanying pain, because there is associated with it the feeling that this pleasure may not be sustained in the future.

- You turn your feelings on and, if you take credit for them, you can turn them off–that is, control them. However, be careful not to suppress them.

- If you really see the reality of a problem, it is licked.

- You can resolve any problem here and now.

- Every problem is an ego problem. In order to have a problem there has to be an ego-frustration.

- Martyrdom can be ego.

- Suffering is the opposite of godliness.

- Suffering is not spiritual.

- God is joy. Suffering is Satan.

- The more you suffer, the more you will suffer.

- Suffering karmically develops and leads to more suffering.

- Suffering is good when it drives you to God, or to seek your Self.

- Every time you feel miserable, there is present an excellent opportunity to make a big step forward.

- The less we allow our Self to be, the more miserable we find ourselves.

- Feeling sad about anything is holding onto it. Say, "This is something I have to let go of," and immediately you will feel better.

- When you are miserable, you shouldn't try to escape it. Get quiet and go within until you see the reason for it, or better, be your Self.

- If you will take full responsibility for feeling bad, you will feel like a Master.

- Every time you feel restless or unhappy, there is ego-desire behind it. If you can get it up into view, you'll let go of it with a chuckle. It's an opportunity to let go of something that's running you. Look for the ego-motivated desire, and, when you see it, let go of it and immediately feel lighter and happier.

- Every time you drop ego, you experience joy.

- Discover who the sufferer is; on discovering this, you find all joy.

Comments:

Who is the sufferer? Whatever answer comes to you is not it. Who you truly are cannot be described in words. It can only be pointed or alluded to. Discover who suffers for yourself and end all suffering.

In the meantime, every time you experience discomfort it is an opportunity for growth. Most of us on the path do the processes, inner work, or releasing in order to get high. Then we stop and try to coast until the next problem presents itself. That is why the world has to appear to push us from outside of ourselves with difficulties. Our progress would be much more rapid if we would go high in order to do our inner work or release and use every down as an opportunity to go even further.

Suggestions for the week:

There are two other ways to support yourself to make growth an every moment event. Every time you experience what you would call pain or suffering, allow yourself to discover who is suffering by asking yourself: "To whom is this experience?" or "Who is having this experience?" What may arise first is "me" or some intellectual substitute for the Self. No matter what answer arises, ask yourself: "If I am more than that, what am I?" Keep going along this line of inquiry until the illusion of suffering and a sufferer dissolves into the silence of the Self.

The other way to support yourself to move more quickly is to allow yourself to keep going even when you are feeling good. You can ask yourself the question that Lester used, which is: "Could this get any better?" This will lead you to further exploration. You can also use the question: "Could this exploration go any further or deeper—am I missing something?" Either one of these approaches will allow you to go past your usual stopping places. You will experience deepening joy and freedom until you discover that you have always been at rest as the freedom that you were seeking.

You can also explore these polarities:

- Growth is hard–Growth is easy.
- I want to stop–I am willing to go further.
- There is somewhere to go–There is nowhere to go.
- I am miserable–I am happiness itself.
- Could I allow there to be as much suffering as there appears to be? –Could I allow there to be as much happiness and joy as there is?

The next seven pages of this book are designed to help further your own exploration. You can view them as your diary of progress during the week that you are working with this session. Use the space allowed on each page to write down your gains and realizations as they happen, as well as for notes on working with the various exercises.

Day One

Day Two

Day Three

Day Four

Day Five

_____
_____
_____
_____
_____
_____
_____
_____
_____
_____
_____
_____
_____
_____
_____
_____
_____
_____
_____
_____

Day Six

Day Seven

"Marry to help the other one get realization.

Marry only to help the other one fully know

God–that should be the basis for marriage."

Lester Levenson

Session 3

Family Relationships

Why do we marry? Why do we have children? What are we seeking in marriage? In children? The answer to all these questions is: We want the greatest happiness. We believe that in marrying, and in having children, we will be happy. Were that true, all married people would be happy. A mere look at our institution of marriage belies this.

Wherein lies the fault? Is it in marriage? No, the fault lies within us. We wrongly look in the wrong direction. We externally seek happiness outside of ourselves, in others. We shall never find a continuous happiness with no sorrow so long as we look to others or to things outside of ourselves. A happy person is one who takes his happiness from within; he is happy whether married or single. Should we marry or should we not marry? That is a moot question. You will do exactly what you will do. You have predetermined precisely what you will do on this point. Therefore, the important question should be: How can I attain the ultimate happiness?

Marriage affords an excellent opportunity for growth and

should be so used. One is constantly confronted with situations where one may increase one's love for one's family. Every day we should make it a practice of increasing our love, using all the situations we find ourselves in wherein we are not loving to the best of our ability by consciously increasing our love for the other one until it is a completely selfless love. When we reach the state of selfless love, we have reached the Godhead.

Q: What a difficult thing it is to be married, Lester.

Lester: Some people find it very easy. The difficulty is in us and not in marriage.

Q: It has a positive aspect, hasn't it? Isn't there a release from selfishness?

Lester: Yes. Marriage should teach us selflessness.

Q: So, in that way, there is a positive step, if it's handled correctly. It teaches love of one person, therefore you can enlarge it in the family and then on to a larger unit. Isn't that true?

Lester: Yes. It's a positive step wherein you're involved in a situation in which you can learn non-possessiveness. It's a very positive step in that direction. The thing we're looking for in a mate is the thing called love. Love is this Beingness that we are. Love is God. Looking for it in a mate, we never find it. However, if one is married, one should very definitely love his or her mate as much as possible.

When we learn how to love a mate properly, we can love others properly. When we realize what love is, and what we are really seeking, we stop seeking it externally in a mate or in the world, and we seek it within. The very best marriage is to marry God. Could you get a better mate?

Q: Should we be married?

Lester: I don't talk against marriage, I don't talk for it. I want you to have what you want for yourself. A married person can find God but has more obstacles than a single person. A single person can more easily concentrate on the path. A married person is forced to be concerned about his mate and children, if there are children. Now, most people who say, "I'll get married and continue on the path," almost invariably get so involved in their marriage they don't have the time nor the inclination for the path. So, in that sense, it's an obstacle.

Q: Unless you married someone who was searching for it also, wouldn't it be a very difficult thing?

Lester: Yes. The very best situation in marriage would be to help the other one get realization. Marry only to help the other one fully know God—that should be the basis for marriage. And the other one should do the same for you. It should be mutual.

Q: It should really be a spiritual state, not a possessive state?

Lester: Love is a freeing of the other one, not a possessing. That would be spiritual.

Q: How best could you guide children into the path?

Lester: The best thing you can do is to set an example. That's the very best way to teach children–by example. They want to be like their parents. So it always comes back to: If you want to help your children, you must help yourself. Then you'll find out you don't have to consciously do anything. Just help yourself, and you'll see them grow with you.

Q: We have two children, and they're really different. They desired to be our children, and we desired them, right?

Lester: Yes. We often choose parents who have characteristics similar to ours so that we can have a constant lesson in front of our eyes. This is why we find parents so difficult sometimes. If there's anything that I see in you that annoys me, it's because I have it in me. If I didn't have it in me, I couldn't even see it in you.

Because we choose parents who have characteristics similar to ours is one reason why people believe in heredity. (We only inherit our physical appearances.) Every child is so different from every other child. You parents know this, that each one is a completely different individual. And if the present environment and heredity had any appreciable effect, they would be very similar.

Q: A thought struck me that a child is born an absolute stranger to the parents. They don't know anything at all about that child. They are a stranger, and it is up to you to make them love you. It is the amount of love that you pour out that induces the amount that they can pour out, isn't it?

Lester: Yes, assuming that our memories are cut off, and we begin at the beginning of this lifetime. But I have to say no, if you take the history before this lifetime. We keep regrouping together. Attachments and aversions to each other keep us coming together lifetime after lifetime. An attachment between two individuals will bring them together again. Or, an aversion will do the same thing, because an aversion is a holding on by holding off. Attachment is holding them to you; an aversion is holding them away from you. But either way you're holding them.

Q: Lester, as a parent, am I loving the flesh or the spirit of the children?

Lester: You're basically loving your own ego.

Q: Because they're part of me.

Lester: Yes. You did it. You created them. You did that tremendous thing. And you want them to be a good example of you. See? Now, if we love our children, we free them; we allow them to grow, to bloom and come out like a flower does. We don't try to fence them in. We free them and guide them and love them—unattached to them—knowing that they are God's Beings. They are just as much God as I am is the way you should feel. Also, they are going to go through life just the way they have set it out anyway. But you should strive to free them, to feel non-attached. This is a higher love than a love with attachment.

Q: Of course, as you say, you do have to lead them.

Lester: Guide them. And they'll ask you for the guidance if you just free them. But they resent being dominated and dictated to the same way you do, the same way you did when you were a child. They don't like to be ordered around, but they want to learn. They have a natural curiosity; they'll ask you. And if you can start from the beginning by freeing them from the first day, bringing up a child is one of the easiest things to do. They'll follow you. But when you start telling them from the first day what to do and what not to do, they behave like an adult does when being told what to do and what not to do. They resent it. They oppose it. Then, oppositional patterns are set up, and by the time they're able to walk around, they've got this oppositional pattern well-developed.

That's what makes bringing up children so difficult. Because of all our attachment, we're trying to steer them, and they resist. We were trained that way; we train our children that way, and they will train their children that way, and it goes on and on. Training could be accomplished without opposition if it starts right. Show them the possibilities, the alternatives, and let them make the decisions. Then they're working with you from the beginning, and they don't develop oppositional habits.

Families are regroupings of people who have been together before. Strong loves and strong hates bring us together again and again. Our attitude toward relatives should be the same as that toward all Beings. The first place to practice love is at home with the family. We should try to love our family more and more by granting them their right to be the way they are, more and more.

It's a great thing for spiritual growth to resolve relationships with parents (even if they have passed on). Parents present excellent opportunities for growth if and when we try to resolve our differences until there is only a feeling of love with no attachment. Family is excellent for bringing up to us all our reactive automatic behavior, because that is where we developed most of it. Giving unselfish love to a child will develop unselfish love in that child this lifetime, and will condition the child for a most happy life.

The main thing that a child wants from us is love, and we cannot fool a child. Children know our feelings, and that is what they read. We fool ourselves with words, but we don't fool them. When children are contrary, it is because they are seeking to get attention from their parents. In early years, this meant survival: If I am approved of by my parents, they will take care of me, and I, the helpless child, will not die. A child tries to be good to get approval. If that's impossible, he becomes bad in order to get attention. This attention subconsciously implies approval. It becomes an aberrated pattern of behavior.

If you can get to see your parents the way they really are and then love them the way they are, you would be accomplishing tremendous growth. You behave most automatically with parents. You'll find your parental behavior patterns applied to the world. You carry on the automatic behavior patterns set up before the age of six for the rest of your life (unless, of course, you change them).

Normalize your behavior with your parents and family. You've got to see your parents the way they are and accept them that way. Nothing should be blamed on your parents. No matter what they do, you should accept responsibility for what you are. Total non-reaction to parents is close to realization. It doesn't matter how we act as long as the feeling within is love. The attitude is more important than the act. Use this with family.

If we were capable of selflessly loving, instead of being in conflict with children, there would be complete harmony. But it is only because we have lost sight of what selfless love is that we are in this difficulty of opposition between parent and child. Parents want to do wrong, yet want their children to do right. This makes the parent look dishonest in the eyes of the children; it disconcerts them, causing rebellious feelings. A child will learn no better than the parent's example.

Our responsibility toward children, because they cannot take care of themselves, is to feed, clothe, and guide them until they are old enough to take care of themselves. But after children become adults, we should let go and let God take care of them, even though they seemingly can't take care of themselves. They need to learn that they, too, are taken care of if they take responsibility for themselves, or, better, if they surrender to God. The only real difference between children and adults is size and experience.

When parents say "don't," they are instilling inhibitions. When parents say "do," they are instilling compulsions. Both cause feelings of inability in the child. Children we see as an extension of our ego. We should see them as individuals and extend to them the rights we do to individuals.

If you want to help your child, help yourself. Every child is a whole, complete, infinite individual. Seeing truth doesn't belong to married people or single people. It belongs to those who seek and discover truth. Married people can get realization if they are determined to get it. The only happy couples are those with an understanding of truth. They know that their joy is within and not in the other one.

What people are really looking for is love of God. Not knowing this, they look for it in a mate. Once you get the taste of God, it's easy not to marry. You feel no need for a mate. Being married to God, you reach satiety. It's an obstacle to have a mate. It's an added obstacle to have a child. It doesn't have to be; it can be an aid to growth, if we so use it. There is no one married whose unhappiness does not come from looking to the other one for happiness. The only ideal marriage is when each marries to help the other one grow spiritually. The top attainment is to have nothing but love for each parent, each sister, each brother, and each child. Resolve this and you will resolve your relationship with the world.

Comments:

How do you feel towards your family? More pointedly, do you have only feelings of love for your family? Congratulations if you do. You have let go of a lot of attachment and aversion to the world. This will really support you in your self-recognition. If you have any other feelings besides selfless love for them, I highly recommend that you allow yourself to deepen your love for them. As Lester said often, "The freer you are with your family, the closer you are to freedom."

Suggestions for the week:

If you do have any feelings besides love for your family, I suggest that you set it up as a goal to continually deepen your love for them until that is all that you feel. A goal many have found helpful is: "I allow myself to love and support (my mother, father, sister, brother, husband, wife or lover) exactly as they are. I want for them whatever it is that they want for themselves."

Here is another great way to both increase your love for your family and free them and yourself. Make a list of what you like and dislike about each family member and then let go of these attachments and aversions in the following ways. With each like and dislike on the list, ask yourself: "Could I allow myself to like this about (the person) as much as I do?" Then ask yourself: "Could I allow myself to dislike this about (the person) as much as I do?" As you ask these questions back and forth progressively on either a like–attachment–or a dislike–aversion–you will begin to feel it dissolve inside. Keep switching back and forth until you can answer "yes" to either of these questions.

If you are working on an attachment, the completion question is: "Could I let this attachment go?" If you are working on an aversion, the completion question is: "Could I let this aversion go?"

To go even further, take your lists about your family members and do the same exercise by exploring the attachments and aversions that you have for yourself.

Allow yourself to take your exploration even deeper with these polarities:

- Could I allow myself to hate (the person) as much as I do? –• Could I allow myself to love (the person) as much as I do?
- I am not you–I am you.
- Could I allow myself to want to change (the person) as much as I do? –Could I let go of wanting to change (the person) and accept (the person) as he (or she) is?

The next seven pages of this book are designed to help further your own exploration. You can view them as your diary of progress during the week that you are working with this session. Use the space allowed on each page to write down your gains and realizations as they happen, as well as for notes on working with the various exercises.

Day One

Day Two

Day Three

Day Four

Day Five

Day Six

Day Seven

"The unrealized person sees the world as
running him, the realized person sees it as
his own projection and therefore he can run it,
it cannot run him."

Lester Levenson

Session 4

Is There a Difference Between Worldliness and Spirituality?

What is the difference between the divine and the worldly, the spiritual and the material? Is there a difference? Is there a difference between being spiritual and being in the world? There is a tendency for us to separate the two. That is a gross error. There is no difference between the spiritual and the material when we look at it from the viewpoint of truth.

The difference is in our outlook, in the way we see the world. It's the way you look at it, that's all. You may look at it from the ego point of view, or you may look at it from the Self. A realized person sees the world only as an out-projection of himself; therefore, it really is his creation. And as an out-projection, it's like a cinema screen out there with this whole universe projected on it and which, at will, could be changed or withdrawn. To the one who doesn't see the truth, this cinema–this moving picture–seems not self-created and, as such, one makes himself subject to it and becomes a slave to it.

A Master is very much in the world; a Master has his feet firmly planted on the earth, but he sees the basic substance just behind the apparent world as his very own Self. And when he does that, everything is in harmony, everything is perfect.

It's not a matter of separating one from the other, or having one or the other, it's merely seeing the truth of the world. When one does, one is realized. When one doesn't, one is forever shadowboxing with his self-created world of opposition. Both see the world. The Master sees the truth just behind it, and there's nothing but harmony! The unrealized one sees separation and opposition, and there's much disharmony. The unrealized person sees it as a thing running him; the realized person sees it as his own projection; therefore, he can run it, and it cannot run him. Being a Master over it, he resides ever the same, in peace and tranquility, and lives in complete ease all the time.

We must, in our everyday lives, be in that state of tranquility, and, until we can be in that state while in the details of daily living, we haven't reached the top. So, there are no two categories, the world and spirit; it's all one and the same. It's just a matter of the way we look at it. We should strive to get to the place where no one and nothing can perturb us.

When you get to that state, you are at the top. You are in the world, and nothing and no one can disturb you in the slightest. Develop this. Make this a practice. Make this your way of life. Do not react to people; do not become angry, jealous, hateful, and so forth. Remain ever the same, ever the same. No matter what happens, no matter what goes on, you really are ever the same, serene and poised.

Q: But, Lester, when I look at the world, I see differentiation.

Lester: Anytime we see any difference, or a difference between the spiritual and the worldly, it's because we don't have enough understanding of the spiritual as yet. We are separating. The highest state is when we are in the world and in spirit at one and the same time, and there is no difference. When we're there, we don't see it as world and spirit. We see it as one and the same thing. We see a Oneness; we see it all as our very own Self. Or, if we want, we see the whole world as being within us, as a dream is within us in sleep. No matter what happens in the dream, we remain the same. We see absolutely no difference in anything; there's a singular Oneness throughout everything. Nothing changes. Ever-the-same is our feeling.

This can be used as a yardstick to know how far we are on the path. Is everything ever the same? Do things really not change? It is a little shocking when we start examining it from this point of view. How far am I on the path toward seeing the sameness, the Oneness, the no-otherness, the nothing but God, God in All, the God in everyone? When you accomplish that non-duality, you lose the feeling of "I." If you want to recognize the "apparent" others, you use the word "we." But more than that, you would rather talk about yourself in the third person.

That is the feeling a Master has, and he talks that way. Certain Masters will not speak of themselves by name. They'll speak of themselves in the third person as their disciples do. For instance, if everyone called me what Ken jokingly calls me, I would talk about Father Divine. Instead of saying "I," "me," or "Lester," I would talk about him (pointing to himself), Father Divine. That's just the way you feel when you're in the state when all is one and all is the same. You don't identify yourself with just your body. I've been emphasizing this point, because quite a few were asking questions and talking about the two–the world and spirit–not knowing that, in truth, they are one.

Q: There is no difference?

Lester: Right. It's one and the same, when you see it aright. If you see it through illusion, if you see it incorrectly, you'll see separation. You'll see the differentiation that this is spiritual and that is worldly, that this is divine and that is mundane.

Q: The "I's" are our ego?

Lester: Yes. The "I's" are a condescension on the part of a Master in order to communicate with the apparent egos. A Master sees nothing but Masters–specks of infinite light, all looking alike: blazing, effervescent, radiant Beings, points of Beingness all being One. This is the way a Master really sees everyone. He doesn't see people the way we see them.

Q: Does he see them as different shades or all one shade?

Lester: Identical points of light, of one ocean of light–brilliant, effervescent, emanating–with center everywhere and circumference nowhere. Are you trying to imagine what it's like?

Q: Well, I had an experience of seeing something like that, and it's a light like a bright sun.

Lester: Yes. A bright, blazing sun. Masters can see nothing but a

Master in us. At the same time, they can go through the pretense of seeing it otherwise, by saying, "Harry, yes, you do have problems," or, "Harry, you do have a body, and you do live in a house." But, as they say it, to them it's like a dream-voice talking, or apparently talking, and it's all an apparency. It's a pretense. They're actually pretending, as their view of the omnipresent, infinite One never changes.

Q: They are pretending a duality then, actually, where we're more or less living it?

Lester: Yes. However, we're pretending it, too, but we don't know that we're pretending it. A Master pretends it, and he knows that he's pretending it. We are ignorant of the fact of our pretense.

Q: In that way he's coming down to our level?

Lester: Yes. And he does it only to help us.

Q: Well, why can't I, as a human being, say, "I will play a game of baseball?" When I say I'm a baseball player, I can make myself subject to all the rules. But I don't have to play baseball. So, why can't God say, "I will play the game of being Bob?" And then He puts Himself subject to the limitations of Bob as He defines it, as when I play baseball, I make myself subject to the rules.

Now, why can't God, to entertain Himself, be a Bob? Or be a Lester, and be limited, in a sense? The thing is, if I play baseball, I limit myself to all the rules of being a baseball player. Well, then I will play baseball and have a good time and be Bob.

Lester: God can, and does, but He never forgets He is God! Do you never forget?

Q: Therefore, I am God who is playing Bob, and, for the moment, I forgot?

Lester: You only are if you know that, not if you state it. Stating it, lip service, doesn't equate with knowing that.

Q: I agree absolutely.

Lester: So, theoretically, you are right. Now, the important thing is to carry it out practically, to know your Beingness in God while you are playing the game–to know that you are God and that you are pretending to be limited as a body and so forth.

Q: And any time I don't want to, I don't have to play, and I don't have to take that particular step of being limited, because I am the creator of the game. I make the rules, and I don't have to play any more than I have to play a baseball game. I can quit just like that (finger snap)!

Lester: That's the way it is. All right now, when you don't really know that you are God, you can discover it by tracing the source of "I." If we trace the source of the ego, "I," we'll discover it's the infinite Being. If you'll trace the source of the mind, you'll discover the same thing. The infinite Being is putting this pretense of limitation, ego, and mind over itself so that we don't see this statement of truth: that this world is only God playing a game of apparent limitation.

The way to discover it is to seek the source of the ego, "I," and, if we stay with it, we'll discover that it is really the Infinite I that I am.

Q: Well, according to you, if I play the game of ball looking up to God, then I don't have it made. If I do anything at all looking out from God, then I know who I am. But if I play the game looking up to God, from the outside, then I don't know.

Lester: You are very right. Translating that into Christ, if I look up to Christ, or believe in Christ, that isn't it. I have to look out through the eyes of a Christ. I have to believe as Christ believed; I have to be as a Christ. I'm just taking what F said and putting it in a biblical way.

Q: It's in what you say. I read it in the Gita this morning and also in what you say, so you get your stuff from a good source.

Lester: I always start with stating that this knowledge is not mine. It is truth: I can't make it, I can't unmake it. I can recognize it or not recognize it. That's the choice that we have, to recognize the truth or not to. We can't make it, we can't do anything to it–but we can recognize it.

Q: All the books that I read say the same thing: Patanjali says it, Yogananda says it, the Gita says it, and the Vedas say it. They all say it.

Lester: And they said it a thousand years ago, a million years ago, a billion years ago, a billion, billion years ago; and in the future they'll say the same thing. Because truth is that which never changes; It is changeless. The basic truth will never, ever change in all eternity, and you can know this for the entire universe.

If somebody comes from a planet billions and billions of light years away and tells you otherwise–no matter how high he looks, acts, and talks–if it doesn't fit in with what you know of the changeless truth, you can be sure he's wrong, even though he's acting and looking like a god.

Do you know what I'm saying? Even if an angel tells you something, if it's not in accordance with truth, reject it, because there are so many high-appearing Beings that look like gods that you can be very easily fooled–until you know the truth. Truth is the same throughout, from infinity to infinity.

Q: We're trying to get ahead as quickly as we can, and we listen and read, and we think the right thing to do is to be on the path–but I go to church, and I see a priest or a monk up there, and he's been struggling on the path for twenty years. How can I make it quickly when I see in front of me someone who has been on the path much longer, and he's struggling?

Lester: All right, look at it this way. If you want to go from Los Angeles to New York City and the direct route is not known to you, you start probing. You might go up to Washington State first, then cut eastward, then come down to Nevada, then go up to Montana. However, if you know the direct route, you take the direct way and get there much sooner. Probing may take you a whole lifetime. Going directly, you could do it in three or four days' time.

Q: Don't say another word to me, because I got the answer.

Lester: All right. Now, the priest or monk doesn't see the direct route, and he's probing and he's learning bit by bit. He'll get to New York eventually if he keeps trying and wandering all over the United States.

Q: But doesn't each of us have different abilities? One person gets over something very easily, very quickly, and someone else has a problem that's deep-seated, and it's been with him a long while, which takes a very active struggle to get over?

Lester: Yes. However, quickness of realization is determined by the intensity of the desire for it. How far have we gone in our desire for it? If we've gone very far, the realizations come fast and easily.

Q: And we stick by them then?

Lester: Yes. They really stick with you. I say to you: I'm not teaching you. You're getting something you've known. You are doing it; you're just re-remembering things you've always known. I can't give you this knowledge; no one can. I just suggest, and you open yourself up to that which you already know, have always known, and always will know, subconsciously.

Q: In other words, you just read a page of your true Self. Well, it's Self-realization, actually.

Lester: Yes, and this is also true: If you haven't grown much, or as much as someone else, you can go way beyond that one if you have a very strong desire for it. Only a very strong desire for full realization will give it to you this lifetime. Anyone who has only a desire for truth will get full realization quickly. You can override your past conditioning when you want to. How long should it take an infinite, omniscient Being to know that he is omniscient, omnipotent, and omnipresent? How long should it take him to do that?

Q: One realization.

Comments:

Do you see the world as you? Do you see it as your creation? Would you want to change any part of it if you clearly saw the truth of it being merely an image in your mind? Allow yourself to explore the possibility that there is nothing separate from the truth of who you are. The more you explore this idea the more it will dissolve, revealing that which is beyond the world of ideation.

Suggestions for the week:

The following exercise can be done as you appear to move through life or you can take specific times to explore it exclusively. Allow your body to be in motion as it is, and then allow yourself to shift gently between the two following perspectives, engaging yourself as fully as you can in each. Let yourself hear, see, and feel what it is like to explore the statements while you go about your activities. "I am in this scene–This scene is in me." As you do this, you will move beyond the usual boundaries that appear to confine you.

You may also want to explore the following polarities:

• I am me–I am blazing, effervescent, radiant Beingness.

- I am here–I am centered everywhere with circumference nowhere.
- I am in the world–The world is in me.
- I am constantly changing–What I am has never changed.

The next seven pages of this book are designed to help further your own exploration. You can view them as your diary of progress during the week that you are working with this session. Use the space allowed on each page to write down your gains and realizations as they happen, as well as for notes on working with the various exercises.

Day One

Day Two

Day Three

Day Four

Day Five

Day Six

Day Seven

"The more we develop love, the more we

come in touch with the harmony of the universe

and then our life becomes more beautiful,

more bountiful and more delightful."

Lester Levenson

Session 5

All About Love

I thought tonight I might talk on the subject of love. Love is one word I don't often use, mainly because it's so misunderstood. I also believe that only through growth do we understand what love is. Defining it, we just add some more words to the usual words, and it doesn't really convey the meaning. But love is an absolutely necessary ingredient on the path. If we ever expect to get full realization, we must increase our love until it is complete.

Now, the love I talk about, of course, has nothing to do with sex. Sex is a body gratification. However, most of us confuse it and tie it in with love. When you see what sex is and what love is, you'll see that they are two different things. They can be tied together and also they don't have to be. The love that we talk about is the love of Jesus Christ. It's the love complete, which expressed in the extreme is, "Love thy enemy."

I think the best definition of the word is, "Love is a feelingness of givingness with no expectation of receiving for the giving." It's a very free giving, and it's an attitude that is constant. Love doesn't vary–not the type of love we're talking about. The amount we have, we apply to everyone. We love our family as much as we love strangers. This might sound odd, but this is the truth. To the degree we're capable of loving strangers, to that degree we're capable of loving our family.

The concept of possession is just the opposite of the meaning of love. In love, there is never a holding onto, a fencing in, or anything like that. Love has a sense of freeing the ones we love. When we are giving in our attitude, we want the other one to have what the other one wants. I guess the best example of this type of love is the love of a mother for a child. A mother will sacrifice and give everything to the child, without considering herself.

There are other definitions for love. I think acceptance is a good word. When we love people, we accept them as they are. If we love this world, we accept the world the way it is. We don't try to change it, we let it be. We grant the world its Beingness the same way we should grant every other person his or her Beingness. Let them be the way they want to be; never try to change them. Trying to change them is injecting our own ego. We want them to be the way we would like them to be.

Identity is another definition. Love is a feeling of oneness with, of identity with, the other one or all other ones. When there is a full love, you feel yourself as the other person, and you treat the other person just like you treat your own Self. There's complete identity. A constant state of gratitude accompanies a state of complete love. We are thankful for everything. We even thank God for the bad as well as for the good. To understand this requires reaching the state of high love. Only then does thanking God for the bad have any meaning to us. The practical aspect of this is that the more we practice being in a state of gratitude, the more loving we become.

Try this and learn the truth of it. Love is not only a feeling, love is a tremendous power. This is so little understood in the world. We have an example of this type of love being expressed today by Martin Luther King. No matter how much he's attacked, he will give out nothing but love to his attacker. He teaches non-violence. And the greatest demonstration of this type of love was Mahatma Gandhi's winning a war against Britain. He did this without any arms and through his teaching, when he said, "The British are our brothers. We love the British. Non-resistance to the British and to the British soldiers, only love for them."

Gandhi well understood this and was able to win over enough followers in India to make this effective. The power behind love, without question, is far more powerful than the hydrogen bomb–that is, once you know what love is. Love is the most powerful force in the universe when expressed as love really is, not as we have been taught to think of it. It is said that God is love, and I add, "One with God makes a majority."

One individual, with nothing but love, can stand up against the entire world, because this love is that powerful. Love is nothing but the Self that we speak of. Love is God. When we are only love, we are God. To quote the Bible, "God is love. God is all powerful." So, there's some authority for what I'm saying besides my saying it. Love will give not only all the power in the universe, but also all the joy and all the knowledge.

Now, how do we make this practical? The best way of increasing our capacity to love is through wisdom, understanding. Also, we can do things in our everyday life that will increase our love. The first place to practice love is at home, with the family. We should try to love our family more and more and more. I think everyone knows the wonderful experience of love, of loving one person. Can you imagine what it's like if you loved three billion people? It would be three billion times more enjoyable! Home is the first place to keep trying to increase our love for the ones around us by granting them their Beingness. That's the most difficult thing, I believe, to do in a family, especially if the other one is a child. But every child is a whole, complete, infinite individual and a child of God. Next, after loving the ones in our home, we should try to love our neighbors, then our larger group—our state, our country. Then we should try to love all people all over the world.

Q: The Russians?

Lester: Even Russians.

Q: The Chinese, too?

Lester: I heard Oral Roberts say something on that some Sundays ago. He said, "People ask, 'What would the attitude of Jesus be toward the communists if He came back today?'" And he answered, "He wouldn't be the way people expect. He wouldn't have anything against anyone. He would not hate the communists. He would talk against doing wrong, doing evil, but He would never say anything against any human being."

I believe that if we understood the power of love, and that if the majority of Americans loved the Russians, Russia would be won over by the Americans without any arms. After we learn to love all the people in this world, there are many more people outside of this world. I think loving all the people in this world would allow us to meet with our brothers and sisters of other worlds, because in this universe there are many, many mansions–many, many places of abode. And because of our inability to love on this planet, we have cut them off.

So, to come back to the point of being practical: The more we develop love, the more we come in touch with the harmony of the universe, and then our life becomes more beautiful, more bountiful, and more delightful. It starts a cycle going where you spin upwards. Love begets love. Love falls in love with love! There is another thing. If we want to be loved, the way to get it is to love. It is not only the very best method, but it is, I think, the only method.

To receive love, we must love, because what we give out must come back. Looking for love without loving does not bring love to us, it does not satisfy us. This is a basic error in many, many people's thinking. They go through life wanting to be loved, never feeling that they are even when they are really getting the love. The feeling has to be in us. If I love you, I feel wonderful. If you love me, you feel wonderful. It's the one who loves who feels great. So wanting to be loved is getting into a direction that can never be satisfied. The happy one is the one loving, the one giving. Blessed is the giver because he's so much happier.

Love should be felt equally for all. When we say we love one person more than another, if we would trace it through by going inwardly, we would find that the one we love more is a person whom we think we need, who has something that we would like to have. Therefore, we say we love that person more.

Actually, love cannot be chopped up. If you want to test your own state of love, look at your enemies. This is the real test. Or, if you don't want to go that far, look at strangers. Examine your attitude toward strangers. It should be one of: they are me, they are my family. Every mother is my mother, every father my father, every child my child. This is the attitude we achieve through understanding. This is the real sense of the word love.

Q: Lester, it seems to me you're talking about love as giving, giving of yourself and so forth, and yet the conflict that I have occasionally is that it seems that as you give of yourself, people tend to take more and more. And eventually, if you don't put a stop to it, they bleed you dry emotionally, mentally, financially, and they use you as a crutch.

Lester: That's impossible, if we feel the real love. If we have the correct attitude of love, that doesn't happen. What you're saying, I often hear. What is needed is for us to know what real love is. The givingness is an attitude. We can always maintain an attitude of love. Most people who give are not giving lovingly. They're giving because of the recognition they think they will get for giving: "Look at me; I'm doing good," or "I may get my name in the paper," or something like that. You see, that kind of love will get us into trouble. People will drain us on that, because we're looking for something in return. We're looking to put ourselves up in the process; therefore, they'll pull us down.

Q: Don't you think it's easier to love somebody five thousand miles away than somebody next door to you?

Lester: The easiest thing in the universe to do is to love everyone. This is what I think. This is what I've discovered. Once we learn what love is, it is the easiest thing to do. It takes tremendous effort not to love everyone, and you see the effort being expended every day. But when we love, we're at one with them. We're at peace, and everything falls into line beautifully. The main thing is to know love in the sense that I'm defining it, then those things don't happen. But when we love in the sense that humanity understands the word, then you're right. But I don't call that love.

Q: What do you call it? Or do you have a name for it?

Lester: Selfishness, actually. We are doing things really to help ourselves. And yet in the real love, in the spiritual love, there's no self-abnegation. We don't have to hurt ourselves when we love everyone, and we don't. When we love, there's a feeling of mutuality. That which is mutual is correct. If you love, you'll hold to that law, and therefore people won't take advantage of you.

If you are loving, you're applying the most powerful force in the universe. But it's the love of a Jesus Christ I'm talking about, not the everyday selfish love. Practically speaking, if people are trying to hurt you, and you just feel love for them–if they continue, you will see them hurt themselves. If they continue further, they'll hurt themselves more. They won't be able to oppose you anymore. But we have to practice this love that I'm speaking of, not the love as we have known it.

Q: It's a basic attitude. It's nothing you physically or even mentally do?

Lester: It's a constant attitude that evolves in us when we develop it. However, we should try practicing the love, as I said before. First, on our family. Grant everyone in the family their own Beingness, if you can. If you can't, keep trying–keep trying until you can. Then apply it to friends, then strangers, then everyone. By doing this, you will develop it, although it isn't something you can turn on just like that.

Q: In a way, all of us have it, but it's just layered over by many attitudes?

Lester: Yes, it's smothered by wrong attitudes. Now, this love I talk about is our basic nature. It's a natural thing. That is why it's so easy. The opposite takes effort. We move away from our natural Self and smother it with wrong attitudes.

Q: Isn't love almost like a selfishness–because when you love somebody, it's such a wonderful feeling for you?

Lester: Well, this is a matter of semantics. The way you put it, yes, but not in the general sense.

Q: I know when I love somebody, I feel so good. It's such a wonderful feeling.

Lester: It's true after you discover what love is. It's the greatest thing in the universe. It's the thing that everyone wants only because it's his basic nature in the first place. Every human being is basically an extremely loving individual.

Q: To understand this thing of joy, is it the same type of thing as when your mind becomes stilled in one avenue of thought, of acceptance of the other person, and therefore the mind is stilled?

Lester: Yes. The more we love, the less we have to think. If I'm not loving you, I have to be on guard. I have to protect myself. If I'm not loving the world, I'm always protecting myself from the world, which causes more and more thoughts. It puts me extremely on the defensive. Subconsciously, it builds up year-in and year-out, and then I'm a mass of thoughts protecting myself from the world. Now, if I love the world, the world can't hurt me. My thoughts get quiet; the mind gets peaceful, and the infinite Self is right there. And that's the experience of this tremendous joy.

Q: In other words, it's not the object that brings this out. It's the quieting of the mind that actually lets the Beingness come through a little more, and that really is the love experience, isn't it?

Lester: Yes.

Q: The light shines through!

Lester: Yes. What he is saying is that we take our infinite Beingness, our infinite joy, and we cover it over with thoughts. We take the natural state, which is unlimited, and we cover it up with thoughts of limitation. The thoughts smother this infinite Self that we are. It smothers the capacity to enjoy just being. And so all we need to do is to quiet the thoughts, or rid ourselves of all thoughts, and what's left over is the infinite, glorious Being that we are, which is our natural state.

Isn't that odd? That is our natural state. That's the way we were, that's the way we're going to be. We are actually that now, but we don't see it. This infinite, glorious Being that we are, being absolutely perfect, can never change. It's always there. We just don't look at it. We look away from it. We look far away from it. What we should do is turn our mind inward and begin looking at it, and the more we look at it, the more we see it.

Everything seems to point to the same direction, does it not? That happens as we get more understanding of what life and the universe are. Everything fits together more and more, and gets simpler and simpler, until there's just one absolute simple called God. God is simple; everything else is complex. The greater the complexity, the further we are from God. God is One and only One–One without a second.

Q: If someone else has a desire, and there's a feeling that if I went along with him that I might lose something, then that isn't love. But if my love is complete in the sense of whatever they wish I wish, then I wouldn't be afraid?

Lester: Yes. There's a word for it today: togetherness. It's a very good word. Doesn't that fit what you're saying? Togetherness?

Q: The thought occurred to me that when I know my Beingness, I can't get hurt, so how can anybody else hurt me?

Lester: That's true. It's impossible to be hurt when we love fully. We only feel wonderful when we love–in fact, we feel the greatest!

Q: If you feel a sense of togetherness with one more than another, then you begin to separate?

Lester: Yes, it is not full love. It's partial love, and the more partial it is, the less good it feels. When we love fully, we love every being. We have nothing but a tremendously wonderful, warm attitude that everything is fine; every person is just right. We see only perfection, and that's the way we see the world. When we hate, we see the same world in just the opposite way.

Q: When you speak of giving, are you speaking of giving things or spiritual understanding?

Lester: Love is an attitude of givingness. When things are given with this attitude, it is love. If I give you something because I want you to like me, that is not love. That is trying to bolster my ego. The greatest givingness is giving understanding, giving wisdom. If I give a meal to a man in poverty, four hours later he needs another meal again. However, if I give him the principle of how to produce a meal, he will never go hungry again.

Let me end with a quote: "Love is patient and kind. Love is not jealous or boastful. It is not arrogant or rude. Love does not insist on its own way. It is not irritable or resentful. It does not rejoice at wrong, but rejoices in the right. Love bears all things, believes all things, hopes all things, endures all things."

Comments:

Think of the last time you felt really loving or in love with a person, a place, or a thing. Now, allow yourself to imagine, as best you can, magnifying this love until it encompasses all supposed others, all places, and all things. This is a little sense of the love that you are and that is always available to you in every moment. Every moment we either choose to embrace the love that we are or deny or ignore it. What do you choose?

Suggestions for the week:

You can easily increase the awareness of the love that you are by doing this exercise. Think of a person–any supposed other. Start with someone that you already feel some love towards. Ask yourself the following question: "Could I allow myself to love this person as much as I do?" Allow yourself to feel the love that you feel for them as best you can. Then ask yourself: "Could I allow myself to increase my love for this person as best I can?" Allow yourself to increase your love for them to the best of your ability. Continue with the second question until you feel you can go no further and are at rest as the love that you are.

Repeat this procedure with another person. Keep this up until you have done it with everyone you know, including the people that you love the least. Also make sure to include yourself in the list of people on whom you do this exercise.

You can also explore the following polarities:

- Could I allow my love to be as incomplete as it is? –Could I allow my love to be as complete as it is?
- Could I allow myself to be as selfish as I am? –Could I allow myself to be as loving and selfless as I am?

You may also want to explore the question: "What is love?" Whatever answer arises, ask yourself: "If it is more than that, what is love?" and, "If it is even more than that, what is love?" Continue along this line of questioning until you are at rest as love and the question no longer arises.

The next seven pages of this book are designed to help further your own exploration. You can view them as your diary of progress during the week that you are working with this session. Use the space allowed on each page to write down your gains and realizations as they happen, as well as for notes on working with the various exercises.

Day One

Day Two

Day Three

Day Four

Day Five

Day Six

Day Seven

"Karma comes to an end when one realizes it as

all in the mind and one is not one's mind."

Lester Levenson

Session 6

Karma

For those who are here for the first time, our method is one of question and answer. The reason why we use question and answer is that it's one of the very best methods of teaching truth. The most effective teaching is individual teaching, rather than group or mass teaching. The knowledge we're after cannot be picked up intellectually, cannot be gotten from books. Were it so that we could get it from books, all we would need to do is to read the books, and we'd have it.

The only really effective teaching is accomplished by the teacher getting the pupil to experience the answer. It's only when we experience the answer that we really understand. This experiencing is also called realizing.

Do you have a question? No? If you don't have any questions, I can always speak on any phase of the subject that you want.

Q: I'd like to know a little more about how karma works, and why it works. I'd like to know what puts it into effect, what starts the wheel. You mention that it's the thought. Knowing that these things do come back to us, naturally we want only good things to come back to us, so we want to send out the right thoughts.

Lester: The word "karma" is a Sanskrit word meaning action. Its general use means action, and the reaction to the action. Other explanations are cause and effect: what you sow, you reap; what you give out comes back to you. Karma is initiated in thought. Thought is the cause, and action is the effect. When we create a desire, we want something. The desire initiates the thought of wanting something. Wanting something causes us to act to get that something. That something does not satisfy us, and therefore, we increase the desire. That goes on and on and on, and we become bound by desire, never able to satisfy it. If our desires were capable of being satisfied, we would have no desires, right?

Q: Would you say that again?

Lester: If our desires were capable of being satiated or satisfied, we would soon lose all our desires. They would soon be satisfied, and we would have no more!

Q: Which is the state to which we should attain?

Lester: Yes, we should attain the state of no desire, no longing. Then we are happy always.

Q: I understood you to say that karma is a law of action and reaction and could be used—not in the sense of punishment for a wrong deed, but as a reward for a good one.

Lester: Creating things we don't like we call punishment. Creating things we do like we call reward. Creation is initiated in the mind. The mind doesn't know good or bad; it just creates. When we create things that are distasteful to us (and we don't take responsibility for the creation), we say we're being punished.

What is karma? To every action, there's an opposite and equal reaction. It's called the law of compensation. It is initiated in the mind. Every thought we have creates a vacuum, and nature immediately moves to fill that vacuum. The pace at which nature fulfills it is also determined by our thought, and every thought is initiated by a previous desire. Since a desire is not real, but is an assumed lack, an assumed agony of need, it can never be satisfied, and it actually becomes stronger the more we try to satisfy it. The only way we can be happy is to let go of all desire. Then we become perfectly content.

Q: So it takes the two. The thought alone without desire won't do it?

Lester: Without a desire, would you have a thought?

Q: Never.

Lester: Correct. You wouldn't have any thoughts without desire.

Q: Well, there are intellectual desires, aren't there?

Lester: Yes, but they are desires. Otherwise, there would be no thought. You desire to be heard; you desire to communicate with people. It might not be a desire for ice cream, food, for things that the body needs, but it might be a desire for approval. So, desire initiates the whole cycle.

Way back in the beginning, it started with a thought of lack. Then there was a desire to fulfill the lack. The desire caused more thought. The thought caused action. Since the action does not fulfill the desire, we increase the desire and action, keeping it going until we are apathetically spinning in an endless cycle, with satisfaction impossible. All our present thinking is initiated by something from the past. Our total feelings now are all from the thoughts and actions of the past. So, all thinking is now motivated by something that has already happened. Action and reaction go on and on that way, and we are caught. It's almost impossible to have an original thought anymore, every thought being based on past thoughts.

Q: So, then, it all started way back when?

Lester: It's beginningless, and it's endless. I'll take you a step higher. Let us look at the example of the rope being mistaken for a snake. You're walking along the road–there's a rope on the ground, and you think it's a snake. Karma is in the realm of the illusory snake. When did that snake begin and when will that snake end, so long as you think it's a snake?

It's beginningless, and it's endless, because, in reality, it never was–it was always a rope. If you are in karma, it is a forever thing. If you are not in it, it never was. Does that make sense? Karma is beginningless and endless. Hence, it's impossible to work out karma. Some schools of metaphysics teach that you must work out your karma. While you're trying to work it out, you are creating new karma for the future, so, it's impossible to work it out.

Well, what can we do? Awaken from the illusion, and you'll see the truth! See the snake as the rope! Once the rope is seen as real, the snake no more is. When we see the truth of our Being, all this action and reaction turns out to be a dream-illusion and therefore, as such, cannot touch us anymore.

Q: Didn't you say we become the observer? I understood that the cycle still must be performed, regardless of enlightenment. Is that correct?

Lester: No, that is, once your understanding is full–from that moment on, there's no more karma. When I say, "Be the witness," that is still in the realm of duality, witnessing the duality, but it's a giant step forward. It's a method of letting go of the ego-sense of being the doer. It's a mode of behavior that's very conducive to growth.

However, when you are fully realized, you'll look at the world, and you'll see only a singular Oneness in everything and everyone. And you'll see that it is all nothing but your very own Self. And the Self is only the Self. So, what happens to the world is that you see it as it really is. You look at it as the rope instead of seeing it as the snake. Then you are out of karma, and there is no more karma.

Now, what's a little confusing to you, are statements that have been made at different levels of approach. Things at one level seem to contradict things at another level. However, when the truth is seen, all contradictions vanish. So, from the highest point of view, when you see who and what you are, there is no karma. When you see your real Self, there's only Beingness; action and reaction are only apparently going on.

Q: Let's say I'm driving out onto the freeway, and I see a guy coming, and I step on the gas and get in front of him. What does this do to me? Is there a reaction coming back from this?

Lester: In this dream-world, to the last ounce, there's action and reaction.

Q: One of the big things with any human, and I know I am no different, are thoughts of sex. This is quite a strong interplay and quite a strong force. How does this all get worked out?

Lester: It's one of the most difficult things to transcend. However, it's possible and it's relatively easy to do it, once you recognize that all that joy that you're seeking through sex you can have all the time—but much more so—once you're out of the trap of desire. That's why I say, "Get to the higher place where, in order to have sex, you give up joy." Then it's an easy thing to let go of.

Meantime, moderation is the best guide. Happiness is only your very own Self; happiness is your basic nature. You don't need anything external to have it. But you think you do, because you've covered over this happiness with layers and layers of limitation: I must have this to be happy, I must have that to be happy. And this has been going on for a long time, but the more you see who and what you are, the less desires have a hold on you.

Q: You have shown the way or method for me by which I have realized that there is something greater than sex. I have now realized that sex is actually a giving up of something, giving up of a higher feeling for a lesser feeling. It's much easier to understand in that light.

Lester: Sex will keep you earthbound. It's necessary to get above it. Having sex will not prevent you from moving toward realization, but while you are enmeshed in it, you are a slave to it and can never get full realization. You are making the physical thing the joy, and it isn't. The real thing is that you are that joy, only a million times more so! As high as the feeling is that you get from sex, you can go way, way beyond that feeling in joy and have it twenty-four hours a day. And it is this unlimited joy that you are really seeking, but you sacrifice it for sex.

Q: When we do things and realize that they should not be done, can we dispose of them by doing the opposite?

Lester: Well, if you're doing the opposite, you're involved in action again, creating the opposite for the future.

Q: You just have to be desireless?

Lester: Yes, that's it! Being desireless, you will see who and what you are. You'll see that you're above all this illusion of karma, and then it can touch you no more.

Q: When you do see that, the release is so tremendous, it's like a sex release.

Lester: Much greater, much greater. I'll have to get some testimonials for you, I believe. (Laughter)

Q: If you drop the desire for something, will it still come your way?

Lester: No. The desire is the cause for it. You can mentally undo karma by mentally undoing desire. Karma is caused by desires that remain in the subconscious mind. Dropping desire drops all thoughts of it. If you take desire out of the subconscious mind, the seeds of karma are no longer there. This is the fastest, the very best way of undoing karma. If you want to undo karma, do it mentally. Why experience it again and again and suffer it? If you let go of things mentally, you let go of them forever; then you don't have to experience them. As Jesus said, "Whosoever looketh on a woman to lust after her hath committed adultery with her already."

The act originates in the mind. Every negative thought, every bad thought we have, creates karma that we don't like, and we call it bad karma. If people only knew this! It doesn't matter whether we carry out the act or not. The seed is sown in the thought.

The remainder of this session is composed of aphorisms taken from various other talks by Lester. Allow yourself to take as much time as you need pondering each one before you go on to the next.

- Karma sows the seeds of its own destruction.

- What we go through is determined by what we have gone through. This is the law of compensation or karma. In between physical bodies, we choose a certain part of what we have been through to go through the next time around. We set up similar situations, hoping that this next time we will transcend them. You always get another opportunity, ad infinitum.

- Bad karma keeps us so miserable with negativity that we

change our bad karma to good karma, and that turns out to be a golden chain instead of an iron chain. Freedom is above karma.

- Whenever we move up, something happens to test us. What actually happens is that we subconsciously feed ourselves more karma, because we have become stronger and can face it.

- Karma is nothing but the accumulated past habits of thought that are going on subconsciously.

- Karma is the conglomeration of all the subconscious thoughts running you. Get rid of these thoughts; quiet the mind totally, and there is no karma.

- Where is karma? It's in the world of illusion.

- Anything karmic is really comic.

- Karma is a harmer. It is a bondage maker.

- We hurt ourselves when we judge others, because it is karmic and returns to us.

- The fastest way out of karma is to grow.

- Karma and reincarnation are part of the illusion and have no part in the reality. Past lives should not be gone into as it is playing with the unreality, making it seem more real.

- Get to accept karma. The idea that you can fight it is contrary to the accepting of it. If you accept it, your fears, frustrations, tensions, miseries, etc., are alleviated, and you are no longer holding onto it by attempting to avert it. Since there is nothing you can do about it, you just let it be. Everything this body is going to go through, it will go through. Understand this and remain as you really are–free.

- You can't change what the body will go through. That was determined by you by prior action. However, you can choose not to be that body, but to be your Self.

- The ego doesn't like to hear that it doesn't have free will. But the ego itself is a product of karma.

- Examine karma, and you will discover that karma and destiny are one and the same.

- Acts performed with no interest in the fruits thereof produce no karma.

- If action is being done without attachments and aversions, there is no karma being created.

- Once you reach the state of non-attachment, you can enjoy the world and do it without creating any karma.

- It is when we rise above karma, good and bad, that we move into being our real Self.

- How can an infinite Being be subject to karma, karma being an extreme limitation?

- Get above karma; don't work out karma.

- Karma comes to an end when one recognizes that it is all in his mind, and he is not his mind.

- There's one act that will do away with all karma: be your Self.

- All actions that the body will perform you have already concluded before it came into existence. The only freedom you have is whether or not to identify yourself with the body and its action.

- If an actor plays the part of a king or a beggar, he is unaffected by it, because he knows he is not that character. In exactly the same manner, we should carry out our part in the world—and whether we are king or beggar, we should be unaffected by it, knowing that we are not that character but are a grand and glorious Being, our very own infinite Self.

Comments:

Letting go of desire is the key. The more you let go of desire the more you are free to just be in this moment, free from anticipation or dread. There is nothing wrong with having as long as you recognize that everything is on loan from God. Thank you, God, for all your bounty! If you desire anything, desire for things to be exactly as they are and for you to wake up from the illusion of "me."

Suggestions for the week:

Since desire is what motivates all thought, allow yourself to start exploring the underlying desires that are motivating your thoughts. As you move through life, occasionally pause your mental activity long enough to ask yourself this question: "What is the desire that is motivating these thoughts?" If you do this with an open mind and heart, the motivating desire will present itself and you can let it go. In order to support yourself to let it go, ask yourself: "Could I let go of wanting (the desire)?" This is especially helpful when you find that you are feeling disturbed or your mind is particularly active.

The more you let go of desire, the quieter the mind will become and the more you will rest as the freedom that you have always been.

You may also want to explore the following polarities:

- I am subject to karma–Karma is for the body that I have never been.
- I have a past–There is no past, there is only now.
- I have a future–There is no future, there is only now.
- Karma is real–Karma is only imagined.

The next seven pages of this book are designed to help further your own exploration. You can view them as your diary of progress during the week that you are working with this session. Use the space allowed on each page to write down your gains and realizations as they happen, as well as for notes on working with the various exercises.

Day One

_____

_____

_____

_____

_____

_____

_____

_____

_____

_____

_____

_____

_____

_____

_____

_____

_____

_____

_____

_____

Day Two

Day Three

Day Four

Day Five

Day Six

Day Seven

"The stability of one's peace is the best

measuring stick for one's growth."

Lester Levenson

Session 7

Growth and Receptivity

Happiness per se is not necessarily an indication of one's state of realization. Aborigines and natives are as happy as we are and sometimes more so. We who are supposed to be at the upper end of civilization, as a whole, might not be as happy as they are. Their enjoyment is mostly through the physical senses. Our enjoyment is more through the mind; hence, we are capable of more joy.

However, because this allows more joy, it therefore allows more misery. Many of us think that the things we do that give us a state of happiness are giving us spiritual growth and therefore are the right things to do. This could be true, and it could also be false. The happiness we get from a new realization is definitely growth. We are delighted in the new revelation, because we have become a little freer and therefore permanently a little happier.

However, the happiness we get from avoiding or escaping unpleasantries is not growth. Rather than furthering our growth, it keeps us bound to the unpleasantries we are avoiding. Until they are faced, looked at, and dropped, they will remain in our subconscious and emerge from time to time until we finally drop them. Therefore, in order to be undone, they must be faced and not avoided. Then no escape is necessary. However, it's really true that the greater our growth, the happier we are. We gain an accumulative total happiness that doesn't vary from day to day. It is freedom from the constant nagging of our compulsive subconscious thoughts. It's a sense of well-being, a sense of security, of peace. Even when things are outwardly being expressed against us, when the world seems to turn against us, we still feel a greater peace within than we did before.

It's that inner state that should be used as a measure of growth. A miserable person can, for the time being, for the moment, be laughing happily. But you cannot use that as an indication of that person's constant state of freedom. How can we tell a person's state of freedom or happiness? By checking when everything is against one. Use this as a method for checking yourself. When things go wrong in the world, then check your state of happiness.

Q: Aren't we inclined to be almost irritated when we see someone else who is happier than we? Maybe it's a little jealousy?

Lester: Yes, it is called jealousy, and when we see one who's happier than we are, we don't like it. Sometimes we attack that one indirectly, even if that one is our mate. This goes on between couples as they grow. When one moves ahead, the other unconsciously resents it, does things to try to undermine the first one. It's motivated subconsciously, but sometimes it does become conscious; even when it is conscious, we sometimes don't understand why we're doing it.

The reason is that whenever two people get together, the higher one automatically tries to lift the lower one up a bit, and the lower one tries to bring the higher one down a bit. They move toward each other. This is an unconscious behavior that goes on whenever two Beings meet. To come back to what I was saying before, the stability of one's peace is the best measuring stick for one's growth: peace under circumstances not ideal, and peace under circumstances in which the individual is being tried. If you maintain your peace while everything out there is going against you, then you really have it. This peace that I'm talking about is the real happiness, and it can be measured by its imperturbability.

If a person cannot be disturbed in his peace, he's got it! He has let go of much ego, because only the ego can be disturbed. The Self of us can never be disturbed. And when we abide as our Self, we allow the whole world to be as it is.

If you want to know your state, check yourself under adverse conditions. Measure your growth by the bottoms, not by the tops. You'll find that your growth goes in cycles, up and down, but that the bottoms keep rising. You should get to the place where the bottom is happiness, and that makes the top even higher–a state of serenity, tranquility, bliss–all with a deep, imperturbable peace.

Q: Where is this bliss, joy, and peace felt?

Lester: People feel it in different places. Actually, it's at the very center of your Beingness, wherever that center may be. This is the first time this series that the group has reached the state of spillover joy. During each series of the past, we had gone from a low point at the start to a very high point at the end.

Q: Do you know why?

Lester: Yes. This is something I'd like to explain to you. Why go down? We're supposed to be intelligent people. We know the way, why go down? That's somewhat stupid when you know how to be high and happy the way you feel now; in fact, it's stupid not to be the way you are now all the time.

The reason why you go down after I leave you is that you have not undone enough of your unconscious thoughts. I direct you toward the infinite Being that you are. As you see it, you undo the contrary thoughts and feel freer and higher. After I leave, the remaining unconscious thoughts of limitation re-emerge, take over, run you, and you feel lower. What is necessary is that you continue to eliminate the unconscious thoughts until there are no more, until you are totally free. Only then will you be satisfied.

I'm pointing out now what you need to do to further your growth. The intellect is excellent for growing and is necessary at the beginning. It sets you in the right direction, it takes you forward. Then you reach a place where it can take you no further. So, what do you do? Do you stop at the top of the intellect, or do you go on? I'm saying let's go on! This doesn't mean let go of your intellect, forget it, or suppress it. No, I'm saying go beyond it. I'm suggesting another giant step forward.

I'm trying to get you to see what this next step is by first telling you what it is not. It is not intellectual. Intellectually, there's nothing more I can give you. What is it? It is becoming aware of your Self by actually experiencing your Self. I could lead you much higher than we've ever gone before if you would draw it out of me. This would help you to experience a higher state than you have ever known before. Then the experience would be your knowledge, and after you experience it, it would leave you with a stronger desire for freedom, a stronger incentive to move faster toward the goal.

Now, I don't want to talk in riddles or intangibles. What is it that will draw out more than the intellect has drawn out so far? It's your state of receptivity. It determines the amount of the power that flows into you. Stated another way, it is letting go of your reservations. As you become more receptive, more of the power flows through me into you and lifts you to the place where you experience your Self. I, Lester, do not do it; it flows through me to the degree that you receive it. It can help lift you to a higher state; by experiencing that state, you definitely know it. You better know that "Thou art That."

Q: How do we do that?

Lester: Greater acceptance of the direction coming through me, and of the fact that happiness really lies within you and not without. The direction up to now has been to quiet the mind by looking at and letting go of subconscious thoughts. As you let go of these thoughts, you become freer, your mind is quieter, your real Self is less obscure, and you're more able to be the real Self that you are. Also, the more you have this experience, the more you are capable of being drawn into your Self by the power flowing through me into you. This could go on to the ultimate.

You have quieted the mind to quite some degree; there is much more to be done. That's why I asked last time, "Who can sit down and immediately quiet his mind and have no thoughts come in?" If you can do that, you're a Master. To the degree you can quiet your mind, to that degree, you are a Master. But everyone is quieter now than they were. Our next step is to get even quieter. And I say we're not going to get it through intellectualism any more, through bandying words up and back. We're going to get it through a method that directly helps you experience the quietude of your Self.

Q: When you quiet your mind and no thought comes in, then what happens? Is it a blank?

Lester: No, it's not a blank; you have no mind to go blank! You're in the realm of All-Knowingness: you don't have to think anymore, you just know everything, and everything falls into line perfectly–every moment. You operate on a feelingness, called intuition. Everyone in this room has experienced it at times. Mind is nothing but the total bundle of your thoughts–a small part conscious, the major part subconscious and held out of view. Mind is not complicated when you see what it is: it's simply the totality of thoughts.

Q: Isn't it true that subconscious thoughts are thoughts that are not being thought of at the moment?

Lester: No, they're being thought of at the moment, but they're not consciously being thought of. They're subconsciously being thought of at the moment.

Q: So that's the difference between conscious and subconscious thoughts?

Lester: Yes, subconscious thoughts are active right now, but we're not looking at them. Are you consciously pumping your heart?

Breathing? Running that chemical digestive factory you have? Are you doing these things consciously? Well, then you're doing them subconsciously.

Q: I didn't have that in mind, exactly.

Lester: I know, but I want to show you how all the thoughts on the body, even though you're not conscious of them, are active right now. There are many, many thoughts connected with running a body; there's a lot of action going on there. They're active right now, even though we're not conscious of them.

Q: That's automated; that's what I call automation.

Lester: Right. But who is now running the automated action? We are. It was originally useful in that we didn't have to consciously operate the body. Then we lost sight of the fact that we threw this onto automatic; therefore, it is now running us. It's difficult to change it, because we have made it unconscious. As we become aware, we see this and then we change it. We become free of it; we re-establish our control over the body.

Our object is to let go of unconscious thoughts, these habitual things of the past that keep us automatically bound. Every habitual thought is a bondage that takes away a certain amount of freedom, happiness. We must let go of all these old habit-thoughts until we are totally free of them. Then we are liberated, fully-realized Masters.

Q: That's why some words will trigger us. If we hear a certain word, we fly into a madness, or, if we hear something else, we feel good.

Lester: Right! So, our object is to let go of all these subconscious thoughts. We have done a beautiful job so far, through using the thoughts, the mind. Now I'm suggesting that we move on, that we get the mind yet quieter by doing that which does it directly–that is, by experiencing your Self. It can also be done in meditation. I ought to redefine the word "meditation."

When I say meditation, I mean holding one thought to the exclusion of other thoughts, and that one thought should be a question. As other thoughts drop away, the mind gets quiet and concentrated. When the mind is concentrated, you will experience your Self, and it will answer any and every question. It will answer the questions that we need to have answered to show us the way out of the bondages. Now, in meditation, the moment you sit down to quiet the mind, it seems to get noisier, which is natural; the thoughts come up for us to drop, to let go of. And each time we let go of one, that's one less that we have to let go of.

As time goes on and we keep dropping these thoughts, we have less and less to drop. Someday, the mind becomes quiet enough so that we fully see this infinite Being that we are; then, in one lump sum, we drop all that is left. And when there are no more thoughts, we are free, and there is left only our infinite Self.

Q: My mind keeps getting noisier and noisier.

Lester: No, it is just that you are looking more at your subconscious thoughts. You don't get more thoughts, you just become more aware of them. The unconscious thoughts that control you will come up. Every time you meditate, this happens. Through practice, someday you will be able to hold one question, one thought, without other thoughts coming in. When you get that far, you are moving rapidly. When you have dropped all subconscious thoughts, then you know what God is, that your Beingness is He.

Q: I'd like to identify the feeling in meditation. Is it similar to a feeling you get while listening to a fine piece of music?

Lester: Yes, it is one of the nicest and quietest feelings you can have.

Q: Then the process of meditation, as I'm seeing it now, has not at all to do with thoughts, but with identifying with this feeling and allowing it to expand.

Lester: Yes! However, this nice feeling is accomplished by quieting the thoughts. Someday, the meditative feeling will be far more enjoyable than the music was.

Q: I feel that it would be such a tremendous welling up that you would almost explode!

Lester: Well, you won't explode, because you take it on as much as you can accept it. There is such a tremendousness in us that, if it came all at one time, we just couldn't take it.

Q: Is meditation related to receptivity?

Lester: Definitely, yes! The better we are able to meditate, the more receptive we are; and the more receptive we are, the better we can meditate. I'm stressing meditation with the hope of helping us to become more receptive. We should let go of the queer ideas we have about meditation. You don't have to be a Hindu or a yogi; you can be one hundred percent American and be a very good meditator.

Meditation is simply holding one question or thought to the exclusion of all other thoughts—and when that question or thought is on your Beingness, that's right meditation. Before we attain good meditation, we have to work to let go of extraneous thoughts that come in while we're trying to hold one question. Then that one question will be answered, whatever that question is. "What am I?" is the final question. When we get the full answer to that, we are in the ultimate state.

Q: Don't you automatically try to answer that when you ask yourself the question?

Lester: Yes, you do, but your mind cannot. The mind can never give you the answer to the question, "What am I?" Why? Because realization is elimination of the mind, and the mind posing the question is not going to eliminate itself. It's almost like saying, "Eliminate yourself." The mind does not want to eliminate itself. Therefore, when the mind poses the question, "What am I?" the mind will never, in all eternity, give the answer.

This is another reason why the intellect can take us only so far. The mind cannot give us the answer, because it itself is in limitation, in finiteness. The answer is in infinity. The mind can pose the question, "What am I?" and when the answer comes, it's from beyond the mind. It's only by quieting the mind that you will be able to see who and what you are. The mind is the blinding cover over this infinite Self that you are.

Q: But underneath it all, I'm trying to find something to hang onto here. Is it this glow, this feeling?

Lester: Yes. If you will examine the glow, you'll discover it to be a feeling of "I"-ness, of Beingness.

Q: Assuming this feeling that we all get occasionally is our true Being shining through—even though it's a very small part we're experiencing—this is the constant experience we should attain to, right?

Lester: Yes! Make it nothing but that, and that is it. Then there's nothing but the experience of "I, I, I, I, I" all the time, and you are there.

Q: Up until now, I've only had an intellectual understanding of these things, and this is the first concrete experience I've had.

Lester: Well, that's not really so. There was always a feeling of experiencing when you got a realization.

Q: Well, that's what I'm finding out. I've now identified with this glow, this feeling.

Lester: Yes, the glow is the experiencing and is higher than the intellect. It's simply experiencing.

Q: That's the way I want it, because books make it sound awfully complicated. How does that fit in with the Self-Realization Fellowship teachings?

Lester: SRF teachings will say the same thing from a different approach. Their approach is for the majority of seekers. Christianity is in the realm of love, devotion, and surrender to God. So are the SRF teachings. Instead of working so hard to eliminate the ego, they say, "Just surrender to God."

If you really surrender, it's only surrender of the ego. "Thy will, not my will" is simply surrender of the ego. SRF directs you to quiet the mind, mainly through meditation, so that your infinite Self becomes obvious. Its main teaching is its methodology, called Kriya Yoga, an integral method that can be used by everyone. If you understand the overall picture, you'll see that there's no disagreement. I'm trying to get you to quiet the mind, to let go of the mind. Their teaching will end up doing the very same thing, and it's a good balance to have our intellectual, wisdom way and their devotional, love, and surrender aspect. However, you can't really have one without the other. So, approaching it from both sides is beneficial, and we should use every aid possible.

We need it; we're in an earth period that is extremely low. We're having opposition going on all day as long as we associate with the world; therefore, any aid that is helpful should be used. When it comes to aids, there is no greater aid than the actual, wonderfully exhilarating experience of being your Self. Be more receptive–surrender your little self and allow the power of your real Self to flow until it, the power, is the only power flowing through you. Glory in that power! Remain in that power! Remain and abide as your infinite, glorious Self!

Comments:

What are you meditating on? Most of us are meditating all the time without realizing it. Another way to look at meditation is that whatever the mind is focusing on is a meditation. Whatever we meditate on we are focusing our power on and it therefore increases. What most of us are meditating on all the time is our problems or limitations and therefore they increase. If you honestly examine what you focus on all day you will see that what I am saying is true.

I highly recommend that you start tipping the balance of meditation to meditating on the Self or on questions that will lead you to recognizing that which you are. As you tip the balance in the direction of meditation on truth, the power of the truth will be more and more active in your awareness and it will increase exponentially.

Suggestions for the week:

Allow yourself to take breaks throughout the day to just rest as the Beingness that you have always been. If you find this difficult to do, allow yourself to use the process of self-inquiry to quiet the mind enough so that you can just rest. As you allow yourself to rest, you will discover that the more you rest the more you can stay at rest, even when the body is in activity. This will increase until you discover for yourself that you have always been that which is perpetually at rest despite all the apparent activity.

You may also want to explore the following polarities:

• Could I allow myself to be as closed as I am? –Could I allow myself to be as open as I am?

• Could I allow myself to be as reserved as I am? –Could I allow myself to be as receptive as I am?

• Could I allow the mind to be as noisy as it is? –Could I allow the mind to be as quiet as it is?

In addition to "What am I?" you may also want to explore this question: "What is that which is always effortlessly present expressing as bliss?"

The next seven pages of this book are designed to help further your own exploration. You can view them as your diary of progress during the week that you are working with this session. Use the space allowed on each page to write down your gains and realizations as they happen, as well as for notes on working with the various exercises.

Day One

Day Two

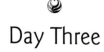

Day Three

Day Four

Day Five

Day Six

Day Seven

The Next Steps

Congratulations on completing Book 4 of *Happiness Is Free*. As you apply what you have learned to your quest for the ultimate happiness, you should find your apparent problems dropping away and your natural freedom shining forth. This will continue until you are at rest in every moment as the Beingness that you have always been and you see the exquisite perfection of All That Is.

The following suggestions are designed to help you get the maximum benefit from the material in this book on an ongoing basis:

1. Allow yourself to use the material in every part of your life. If you only thought about and explored freedom for a few minutes a day, you would gain tremendous benefits. However, if you allowed freedom to be in your mind and heart throughout the day, those results would increase exponentially. Like everything else, the more energy you put into the process, the more you get out of it.

2. Review the material often. Every time you reread and work with the ideas in this book, you will get more out of them. As you mature spiritually, you will understand and be able to apply what you learn on deeper levels. Treat each review as though it were your first time. Explore all the exercises, and allow a full week for each session.

3. Share what you have learned. Communicating these ideas and practices with your friends, relatives, and acquaintances should stretch you and deepen your own understanding. Additional benefits come from surrounding yourself with like-minded people who are also interested in deepening their freedom. However, please remember only to share this material with those who are truly interested in hearing about it. Grant those you know their Beingness—see them as already perfect—whether or not they share your interest.

4. Start or join a *Happiness Is Free* support group. An energetic lift comes "when two or more are gathered in thy name." The larger the group, the more this energetic lift is magnified. Lester used to say that the energy in groups is "squared." In other words, two people have the power of two times two, three people have the power of three times three, and so on. Another benefit of participating in a group is seeing the material from perspectives other than your own. This can deepen your understanding. (See p. 178, Guidelines for *Happiness Is Free* Support Groups.)

5. Read the other four books in this series. Together they comprise a total of thirty-five sessions. Each book, in and of itself, is a complete course on the ultimate happiness. But if you have enjoyed reading and working with this one, you would probably enjoy and benefit from the other books as well.

6. Learn the Sedona Method®. As we have already mentioned, Lester's material truly comes alive when it is combined with the Sedona Method®. Lester was so excited about this part of his teaching that he devoted the last twenty years of his life to perfecting and promoting it. There are two great ways to learn the Sedona Method®. You can explore the power of letting go through live seminars, which are offered worldwide, or in audiotape programs.

To get information on the Sedona Method® Course, you may visit the Sedona Training Associates website: **www.sedona.com**, e-mail us at **release@sedona.com**, or call us at **(928) 282-3522**. At the end of this book there is a fill-out form that you can also use to request further information.

7. Review and deepen your use of Holistic Releasing™. The Holistic Releasing™ process is an integral part of this book. If you have enjoyed working with the polarities at the end of the sessions, you would probably also enjoy our tape programs *Practical Freedom* and *Absolute Freedom* or attending a seminar on this technique. (See the contact information above.)

You are the key to your own happiness. All you need to do is use that key to unlock the secrets of freedom and happiness that are waiting to be discovered right within your own heart. Good luck and enjoy.

Guidelines for *Happiness Is Free* Support Groups

The goal of a group should be to support each participant in gaining the most they can from their use of the material. It is important that a safe space be created so that everyone feels free to participate, yet never feels pressured to do so. This is best facilitated if a different member of the group is given an opportunity to be the leader each time the group meets, if they chose to do so. It helps to prevent one person from dominating the group. It also allows participants to stretch in the direction of helping others.

If anyone brings up an emotional or physical issue that would usually be handled by a trained medical professional, they should be encouraged to seek a health professional. These support groups should never be used as a substitute for competent medical attention. They should be used as an aid to each participant's personal and spiritual growth.

It is helpful to have the support group meet once a week since each session is designed to be used for a full week. If at first that is difficult, meeting once a month would still be helpful.

If you are using private residences for your meetings, it is also helpful to rotate the location where the support group is being held so that the burden for hosting is not borne by only one person. However, if you can find a centrally located free public location we encourage you to use it on an ongoing basis.

The following instructions are for the leader of the support group.

Welcome Everyone

Start with a brief quote from Lester from the week's session. Then allow for a few minutes of silence to give everyone an opportunity to ponder the quote and to get centered and present in the room. Do your best to create the safe space for everyone attending.

Ice Breaker

Have the group share their names and a gain that they have experienced so far from *Happiness Is Free*.

Partner Work

Have each person in the group find a partner and support each other in doing an exercise from the week's session. Select an exercise that would be appropriate to do with a partner from the book. Spend approximately thirty minutes on the exercise, either having the partners switch back and forth, taking turns facilitating each other, or time it so each participant has about fifteen minutes to do their exploration with the support of their partner.

Have each partner open their copy of *Happiness Is Free* to the exercise being explored, so they can remember the verbiage and remind each other to change the wording to the third person using the pronoun "you" instead of "I."

Read the Following Statement Aloud

Be there with and for your partner as best you can. Grant them their Beingness by allowing them to have their own exploration. When you are asking your partner to let go, do your best to let go as you facilitate your partners in releasing. You will find that this happens naturally if you are open to it. Refrain from leading, judging their responses, or giving them advice. Also refrain from discussing the explorations until you have both completed them and you have spent a few minutes in silence. Be sure to validate your partner's point of view, even if it does not agree with your own.

Please refrain from playing the role of counselor or therapist even if you're a trained counselor or therapist. If your partner brings up a medical condition that would ordinarily require a trained medical professional, recommend that they get whatever support they need in this area. If you are not sure whether or not they truly need medical support, you can recommend that they seek professional medical attention, just to be sure.

Have Group Share

Have volunteers from the group share what they got from the exercise. Make sure the group validates their perspective, and support them in letting go and moving up into greater freedom.

Sharing Gains

Give the group another opportunity to share gains if they choose.

Silence

Have the group spend a few minutes allowing their beingness to be in silence.

Thank Everyone for Coming

Thank everyone for coming and encourage the group to maintain the silence within as they go home or go about their day.

Gains from *Happiness is Free:*
Book 4

Please use the space on this page and the next to share your gains from working with this material. If you would prefer you can use a separate sheet of paper or e-mail us at **release@sedona.com** to send us your gains.

Gains from book 4 *continued*

_____

_____

_____

_____

_____

_____

_____

_____

_____

_____

I give Sedona Training Associates permission to quote my
comments in promotional materials and future books. I understand that in exchange I am entitled to receive a discount on the
Sedona Method® Course or the Holistic Releasing™ tape sets.

Signature _____

Name _____

Address _____

City, State _____ Zip or Postal Code _____

Phone _____

E-mail Address _____

WE ARE HERE FOR YOU

Sedona Training Associates is dedicated to helping you liberate your true nature and to have, be, and do all that you choose. Our products have been created for this purpose. To accelerate your progress, we highly encourage you to attend one of our live seminars or purchase a tape program. The following are some of our offerings.

The Sedona Method® Course,

both as a live seminar or as our home study audio program, will show you how to elegantly and easily tap your natural ability to let go of any unwanted thought or feeling on the spot. In addition to gaining deeper awareness of the ultimate truth and your natural state of unlimited happiness, the Sedona Method® can free you to have any or all of the following: more money, better relationships, more radiant health and well being, more effective goal achievement, plus how to break bad habits and other self-sabotaging behaviors, lose weight, stop smoking, and sleep better.

You will also be able to easily, effortlessly and joyously free yourself from stress, tension, panic, fear, anxiety, depression, indecision, low self-esteem and self-doubt, fatigue, insomnia, co-dependency, uncontrolled anger, and grief. In short, you will enjoy living a happier, more productive, more satisfying, more loving and happy life.

The Holistic Releasing™ process, as you have probably already experienced from reading this book, can also accomplish all of the above. It is an integral part of our advanced seminars. You can also deepen your experience of this powerful tool by exploring our Holistic Releasing™ tape programs *Absolute Freedom* and *Practical Freedom*.

Absolute Freedom: This audio set utilizes Holistic Releasing™ to help you to easily recognize and dissolve the barriers that you imagine are keeping you from perceiving your true nature. These recordings will help you to discover the natural state of Beingness that has always been available to you here and now. You will discover that who you are has only appeared to be hidden by your self-imposed sense of limitation. You have always been absolutely free.

Practical Freedom: This audio set is designed to help you to rediscover the freedom to have, be, or do whatever you choose as an alive and practical part of your everyday life. It will help free you to perform at your best in every situation, and live your life with greater ease and clarity. As you apply Holistic Releasing™, you will find that even long-standing challenges dissolve and are replaced by a greater sense of mastery.